EDUCATIONAL GAMES AND ACTIVITIES FOR TEACHERS

SUITABLE FOR ESL

EDUCATIONAL GAMES AND ACTIVITIES FOR TEACHERS

Low-Preparation and Suitable for ESL

DAVID CHASE

DON'T MISS OUT ON THIS FREE TEACHING RESOURCE!

We are delighted to offer you a complimentary and exclusive copy of *"The Big Book of Fun Riddles & Jokes."* This resource is specifically designed to help English teachers make the most of their class time by engaging students in thought-provoking, interactive activities.

We understand that every moment of class time is precious, and that's why we've curated a collection of quick-fire riddles and brain teasers that will encourage your students to learn English while having fun. By incorporating these activities into your lessons, you can create a dynamic and stimulating learning environment that will keep your students focused and motivated.

To access your free copy of *"The Big Book of Fun Riddles & Jokes,"* simply click on the following link:
https://www.subscribepage.com/davidchase. We highly recommend that you take advantage of this opportunity to enhance your teaching skills and inspire your students to achieve their full potential.

If this book has helped you in any way, we'd appreciate it if you left us a review on Amazon. Reviews are the lifeblood of our business. We read every single one and incorporate your feedback into our future book projects .

To leave an Amazon review please visit
https://www.amazon.com/ryp **or scan the QR code below...**

CONTENTS

Preface

The primary goal of a good language teacher should be to teach the language in a practical and engaging manner. Whether the lessons focus on writing, speaking, listening, grammar, pronunciation, or spelling, it is crucial to prepare an interactive and enjoyable class that motivates students to learn.

This book has been created to provide you with a variety of easy-to-follow games and classroom management techniques for you to implement in the classroom. The games that have been compiled in this guide are both entertaining and interesting, they'll also provide a great source of reliable resources for when you need to incorporate some educational fun into your classroom.

Each game has been divided into different categories and subsections to make it easier to select the right game. For example, some will work well for revising vocabulary, and others will be effective for grammar. The guide has also been split up to cater to all types of English language learners, including beginners, intermediates, and advanced learners. You, as the teacher, will be responsible for determining which game is appropriate for the dynamic of the lesson you plan to deliver.

Introduction

Preparation

The key to a successful lesson is always to be prepared. It will improve the quality of your teaching and ensure that your students are learning effectively. Being prepared will give you a clear idea of what you want to accomplish in the class. Additionally, being prepared can help you avoid those uncomfortable moments that teachers sometimes experience when a lesson starts to veer off track. You'll also be surprised by how observant your students are. They are likely to notice if you are unprepared.

Lesson Planning

The most important element of your preparation is to create a lesson plan. Break the lesson plan down and designate a specific amount of time for each task that you will complete as part of the lesson. Creating a lesson plan for the first few times may seem like a time-consuming task, but don't worry, you'll get faster and more efficient with practice. It's a good idea to have a ready-to-use template on your computer. Then it will just be a case of inputting into the template and reviewing the material and choosing which games you would like to use in the lesson.

Types of Games

The choice of game you use will depend largely on the learning outcome you want to achieve in the respective lesson. Certain games may be more effective than others in given situations. This guide has divided the games into the categories listed below, although some may be applicable to multiple categories or levels and can be adapted accordingly.

Warm-up Games

A good way to start a lesson and engage the students is to introduce a warm-up game. Instead of simply asking the students to open their books straight away, a warm-up game can be used to recap a previous lesson or to introduce a new topic. Here, you'll discover some exciting activities that will energize your students and prepare them for the lesson ahead.

Repetition/Drilling Games

Using repetition is essential to help students remember what they've learned, particularly when teaching young learners. Fortunately, there are many enjoyable and easy games that can be used to make repetition a fun and effective way to memorize language.

Team Games

An effective way to engage all students involved is to divide them into teams and play a game. Most students enjoy the competition and comradery, so you can give points to regulate the gameplay and perhaps even offer some sort of reward to the winning team.

Spelling Games

Spelling is a crucial component of learning any language, so it's always a good idea to have some spelling games in your teaching toolbox. However, if you want to keep this type of game to a minimum in your classroom, you can transform some of them into word repetition exercises.

Speaking and Pronunciation

To gain mastery of English it is imperative to practice aurally. These games can help students in correcting one another and to make themselves understood in practical settings. In this category, you will find some interesting games to help your students hone their listening and speaking abilities.

Turn-based Games

These games are typically aimed at advanced learners. Turn-based games are more challenging because they involve progressively complex materials and require individual thinking.

One-on-One Games

You may want to fill up a one-on-one tutoring session with games. It's yet another way to make the lesson fun and interactive. You can find games specifically designed for a single student, or you can adapt games typically used in larger classes.

Basic Level

This section offers a wide range of games, from traditional favorites to new and exciting ones. These games are designed to save you time on lesson preparation while engaging your students in speaking, reading, and writing. Although the games are targeted towards beginners, they can be modified to suit the needs of more advanced learners.

Warm-up

1. *Hangman*

Type: Warm-up

Materials: Marker pen

Probably one of the most renowned warm-up games in the classroom, and one of the most effective for beginners.

Step 1: Think of a word or get one of your students to think of a word and on the board, draw a hangman's gallows and spaces below for each letter of the word or sentence that the students will try to guess.

Step 2: The students should try to guess the word by suggesting one letter or one phrase at a time. If they get the correct letter, write it in the appropriate space. If they are incorrect, write the respective letter on the board so the students can keep track of the letters they have already used. Additionally, add a body part to the hanging man for each incorrect letter given.

---

2. *What Sounds Can You Hear?*

Type: Warm-up

Materials: Marker pen

Step 1: Give the students a few minutes to list as many sounds as they can hear. This activity is great for practicing vocabulary at a lower level. Then ask the students to compare their lists to determine who has come up with the most sounds.

---

3. *Word Association*

Type: Warm-up

Materials: None

Step 1: Seat the students in a large circle. Let one student start with a word that comes to mind. The next student should immediately reply with a related word.

Every subsequent word must be related to the one just prior to it. This can become challenging and requires concentration. The next student in the circle should immediately reply to the last word they heard. The game might go like this:

A: Dog

B: Wolf

C: Forest

D: Tree

E: Owl

Step 2: Ensure that everyone has a turn.

---

4. *Group Dialogue*

Type: Warm-up

Materials: None

Step 1: Have one student start by making a sentence. The next student should respond to that sentence with their own complete sentence as if they were engaging in a discussion between only two people. For example:

A: How are you, Amanda?

B: I am well Liam. How are you?

C: I'm not doing as well as I would like to.

D: What happened?

Step 2: Keep the dialogue going in a normal way until the last students in line conclude the conversation with a realistic-sounding goodbye.

---

5. _Bingo_

B	I	N	G	O
		■		

Type: Warm-up

Materials: Blank Bingo grids

Step 1: Instead of making the bingo grids yourself, have your students make them. Prepare review questions from the textbook or even trivia that your students would most likely know. Each question should cover grammar they have studied before.

Step 2: Hand each student a blank bingo grid and ask them to fill in the grid with the answers to each question. Go over the answers just to make sure everyone has the correct answer. Ensure that no bingo grid is the same by asking students to fill in the answers either clockwise or counterclockwise but each from a different starting point.

Step 3: Now, start the bingo game. Read the questions (not the answers) to get them thinking.

---

6.   *Twenty Questions*

Type: Warm-up

Materials: Picture cards

Step 1: Put picture cards up on the board.

Step 2: Pair up the students and assign a picture to each pair. Have each pair answer only yes or no to each question on the board such as:

Would this be kept outside?

Does it weigh more than one kilogram?

Does it use electricity?

Does it make noise?

Do you have one?

Would you like one?

Can you eat it?

Can you wear it?

Is it used in winter?

Step 3: Students must keep track of the number of questions. Questions can use new vocabulary words to allow students to expand their vocabulary.

Repetition and Drilling

7.   *Simon Says "..."*

Type: Repetition / Drilling

Materials: None

Step 1: Stand in front of the class and perform an action. Begin the game by saying "Simon says…" and then stating what you are doing. The students should repeat after you and do as you do.

Step 2: Choose another action to perform. Have the class mimic you by saying "Simon says …" followed by a description of the action. For example, you might say "Simon says, "Put your hands on your head"."

Step 3: Continue the game by selecting different actions and repeating instructions. The students will learn new verbs while also engaging their whole bodies, which will aid memory retention.

---

8. *Syllable Game*

Type: Repetition / Drilling

Materials: None

Step 1: Write a challenging word on the board. Clap your hands once for each syllable of the word. Draw a box for each clap on the board.

Step 2: Ask students which letters from the word should be in each box, starting with box 1, then box 2, and so on. For example, for the word RETRIBUTION, the letters "TRI" should be in box 2. Test the students' understanding by asking questions such as "Which letters should be in box 3?" and have them answer with the corresponding letters, such as "B U".

28

Example:

Word: R E T R I B U T I O N

Claps: Y Y Y Y Y Y Y Y Y

Box #: 1 2 3 4 5 6 7 8 9

Letters in boxes:

Box 1: R

Box 2: E T R I

Box 3: B U

Box 4: T I

Box 5: O N

Drill: "What letter(s) are in box 3?" Students call out: "B U"

---

9. *Punctuation Game*

Type: Repetition / Drilling

Materials: None

Step 1: On the board, write the following punctuation marks: period (.), comma (,), question mark (?), exclamation mark (!), and apostrophe (').

Step 2: Teach the names of each punctuation mark and have students repeat after you.

Step 3: Speed up and vary the order in which you ask the class to identify the punctuation marks.

10.   *Numbers Game*

Type: Drilling / Repetition

Materials: Marker

Step 1: Write down numbers on the board as follows:

1,	10,	11,	6,	17,	80
2,	20,	12,	7,	18,	90
3,	30,	13,	8,	19,	100
4,	40,	14,	9,	60,	
5,	50,	15,	16,	70	

Review how to pronounce the numbers as a class.

Step 2: Then, form two teams. Let the teacher call out a number, and let someone from each team race to the board and cross that number out with a marker. Each correct number crossed out scores one point.

Step 3: All students should take their turn.

11.   *What Do We Do…?*

Type: Repetition / Drilling

Materials: None

Step 1: Prepare ten nouns and ten related verbs. As an example, decide on ten places and link them to the activities done there.

Step 2: Write all the places out on the board and point to them as your students call out the activities performed there. For example, you might say:

"What do we do in a LIBRARY?"

Library => Read books

"What do we do in a RESTAURANT?"

Restaurant => Enjoy meals

Team-based Games

12. _Pictionary_

Type: Team-based

Materials: Flashcards, hat

Step 1: Prepare flashcards and put them in a hat. Divide students into two groups. Draw a line down the middle of the board to assign drawing space to each team.

Step 2: One member of each team should come to the front and pick a flashcard from the hat. They should draw a picture illustrating the word on the board so that their team can guess what the word is. The first team to shout the correct answer is awarded one point.

Step 3: When the word has been identified, the student who guessed correctly should be the next to draw. The next to go could also be nominated. Make sure, though, that every student has at least one turn to draw. Keep going until all the flashcards have been exhausted.

---

13.   Board Relay

Type: Team-based

Materials: Colored markers

Step 1: At least six students are needed to play this game, but more would be better.

Step 2: Start by dividing the class into teams, with each team consisting of four students. Give each team a colored marker. Write a topic on the board, and below that, assign writing space to each team.

Step 3: Get one student from each team to come up and write down a word related to the topic on the board. Then, the next student in each team should come forward and write another word on the same topic. Keep going in the form of a relay race.

Step 4: Students should write as many related words as possible within the time limit. Teams earn one point for each correct word they write. Illegible or misspelled words do not count.

---

14.   *"Tic Tac Toe"*

Type: Team-based

Materials: Nine prepared questions

Step 1: Divide the class into two groups. Draw a 3x3 grid on the board and number each square. Prepare nine questions and assign one question for each number.

Step 2: Each group takes their turn to call out a number and if they answer the corresponding question correctly, they get the point. For each correct answer, they can place their symbol on the square of the corresponding question.

Step 3: Each group should try to set three of their symbols in a row to win.

---

15.   *Fly Swat*

Type: Team-based.

Materials: Cardboard flies, vocabulary flash cards, flyswatters

Step 1: Split the class in half. Ask one half to go to the back of the class and face the front. Put 20 vocabulary words on a desk in the center and place a cardboard "fly" over 10 of them.

Step 2: Give each team one flyswatter. As you read a passage, have someone from each team come up and swat the fly off the word they heard read from the passage.

Step 3: When a fly is swatted, pause. The one who swatted the fly must spell the word. Give each student a turn.

---

16. *Dictation*

Type: Team-based

Materials: Pen and paper and text excerpts

Step 1: Pair up the students. Each pair must have only one reader and one writer. Place short passages of text on the back wall of the classroom. Have each reader memorize a piece of the text and then run to their partner and dictate it.

Step 2: The writer must write out the text. The first team to finish writing out all the passages correctly wins.

---

17. *Write And Run*

Type: Team-based

Materials: Pen and paper, text excerpts.

Step 1: Divide the class into four teams. Put four copies of a short text on the board. In each team, assign one person as the writer and the rest as runners.

Step 2: The runners should go up to the board, memorize a passage of the text, and dictate it to their writer.

Step 3: When the full text is copied, each team should hand in their writing and take turns reading it to the class.

Step 4: Points are awarded based on finishing times, and points are deducted for mistakes made.

---

18.   *Sentence Kabadi*

Type: Team-based

Materials: Sentence flashcards, table

Step 1: Write out sentences familiar to the students. Cut the sentences up into words and phrases, and then scatter the fragments on a table in front of the class.

Step 2: Divide the students into teams, and have them stand behind a line at a distance from the table. One student per team must rush to the table and arrange the fragments into sentences at the starting count, while repeating the word "Kabaddi" over and over, without stopping, taking a breath only when they have completed the task. If they take a breath before they have finished, they must return to their team and start again.

Step 3: The first team to arrange all the sentences correctly wins. Deduct one point for each mistake in grammar, spelling, or word order.

---

19.   *The Alphabet Game*

Type: Team-based

Materials: Marker

Step 1: Organize the students into lines of no more than five. Then, give the student at the front of each line a marker.

Step 2: Draw a letter of the alphabet with your finger on the back of the last student in line.

Step 3: That student should write the same letter on the back of the person in front of them, and so on down the line.

Step 4: When the students with the markers in front of the line feel the letter written on their backs, they should write any word that starts with that letter on the board.

---

20.   *Invitation To Dinner*

Type: Team-based

Materials: Dinner invitation card

Step 1: Pair up the students and have each pair write a creative dialogue of 30 lines between two speakers about an invitation to dinner. Here's an example of the invitation:

Invitation to the Chamber of Commerce

Prize-giving Dinner

DATE: October 29, 2023

PLACE: Sierra Del Parća Hall, The Firs Hotel, Grayston

TIME: 7.30 PM

ATTIRE: Black tie and black dress

The students have 30 minutes to write out the dialogue.

Step 2: Each pair should take turns coming to the front of the class and presenting their dialogue within 3 minutes.

---

21.   *Name The Place*

Type: Team-based

Materials: 20 flashcards containing place names

Step 1: Divide the class into groups of five. Then, have one member from each group choose a flashcard that names a specific place. In their groups, students should prepare a mini-play based on or set in the place named on the card.

Step 2: Allow groups a few minutes to prepare, and have them present their plays to the class.

Step 3: Instruct the class to guess the name of the place portrayed in each play.

---

22. *Lyric Grab*

Type: Team-based

Materials: A song; music player, and flashcards

Step 1: Choose a song. Select ten words from the song and write them on flashcards. Stick the flashcards onto the board.

Step 2: Divide the class into two lines perpendicular to the board and play the song. When the two students at the front of the lines hear a word from the song that is on the flashcards, they must race each other to grab that word from the board and get to the back of the line as quickly as possible. Only the student at the front of the line is allowed to grab the lyrics from the board.

Step 3: The team with the most flashcards at the end of the game wins.

---

23.   *Spin Zone*

Type: Team-based

Materials: Spinning tops

Step 1: Pair up the students and give each pair a top. Have them spin the top.

Step 2: One student should call out as many new sentences as he can before it stops spinning.

Step 3: Their partner must keep count of the sentences. The student who creates the most sentences correctly wins.

For an easier version of the game, students can say single words instead of full sentences.

---

24.   *Broken Telephone*

Type: Team-based

Materials: None

Step 1: Divide the class into two equal halves and form two lines, ensuring that the teams are of the same size. If there is an odd student, they can act as an assistant.

Step 2: You can whisper the same message to the first person in each group, and then the game can begin.

Step 3: Each student must whisper the message to the person next in line, and the last person in line must repeat it out loud. The first team to accurately repeat the message wins the round.

---

25.   *Word Tennis*

Type: Team-based

Materials: None

Step 1: Divide the class into two teams and write the team names at the top of two columns on the board. Create a middle column where you write categories such as 'ANIMAL', 'CAR', 'NAME', 'DEVICE', etc.

Step 2: Ask the students read out the category names to you. Point to the first student from one group and have them respond with the name of an animal. Then, the first student from the other team must respond immediately with another animal name.

Step 3: The 'ball' then bounces to the other team, and the second student quickly gives the name of another animal. Then the second student on the other team answers.

Step 4: This process continues with each team taking turns to name an animal, without any repetition or hesitation. If a student is slow to answer or answers incorrectly, the other team wins the point.

---

26. *Yes/No Chairs*

Type: Team-based

Materials: None

Step 1: Place a large sign with the word "YES" on a chair and place it at one end of the classroom. Similarly, put another chair with the word "NO" at the other end.

Step 2: Divide the class into two teams and ask a closed-ended question. For example, you could ask, "Can cars run on tomato sauce?"

Step 3: In response, the student must run and sit on the correct chair, depending on their answer. In this case, the answer is 'no'.

Step 4: Once they sit down, they must answer the question in a full sentence, saying "No, cars cannot run on tomato sauce." If they do not, they lose the point, and the other team earns it.

---

27. *Word Searching Game*

Type: Team-based

Materials: Word Search puzzle

Step 1: Create or download a word search puzzle and cut out the words from the puzzle.

Step 2: Distribute the word search puzzles to the students without the words filled in.

Step 3: Call out one word for each team's puzzle and have the students search for where that word belongs. The first team to place the words correctly scores a point. The students must know how to spell the words correctly and count the number of letters in each word.

You can make a fun variation on this by describing the word instead of saying it.

Spelling and Grammar Games

28.   *Auction*

Type: Spelling / Grammar

Materials: Monopoly money

Step 1: Make a worksheet that includes at least 20 sentences using the grammar structures that students have recently learned. Ensure that three of the sentences contain grammatical errors.

Step 2: Divide the class into teams of five, and give them 10 minutes to mark the correct and incorrect sentences.

Step 3: Provide each team with the same amount of money. Then, read out the sentences at random and auction them off one by one. The students should only bid on the correct sentences. As the students bid, the auctioneer should sell each sentence to the highest bidder. The winner will be the team that ends up with the most correct sentences.

---

29.   *Verb Review*

Type: Spelling / Grammar

Materials: None

Step 1: Allow the students five minutes to review the verbs they have learned.

Step 2: Write a sentence on the board, such as: "Actions we do with perform with our hands".

Step 3: Then, give all the students exactly one minute to write down all the verbs related to this sentence, such as "work," "type," "gesture," etc.

Step 4: When the time is up, students should count the number of verbs they have listed. For each correct verb, the student earns one point. However, if a verb is repeated, one point should be deducted.

---

30. *Create Your Own Similes*

Type: Spelling / Grammar

Materials: Flash cards with adjectives

Step 1: Write down twelve sentences containing similes on the board and underline the similes in each sentence. For example: "The man is as tall as a giraffe."

Step 2: Each student can pick a flashcard with an adjective and create a unique and creative simile for that adjective in a sentence. The simile should make sense logically. The funniest or most original sentences will earn the highest points.

---

31. *Seat Swap*

Type: Spelling / Grammar

Materials: Flash cards

Step 1: Have students sit in a circle. Lay a pile of flashcards face down in the center of the circle.

Step 2: Have a student pick up a flashcard and make a sentence with the word on it. When the sentence is grammatically correct, call out "SWAP" and remove one chair.

Step 3: The students must immediately stand up and find another seat. One student will be left standing. That student must then pick a card and make a sentence with it.

---

32.   *Disaster*

Type: Spelling / Grammar

Materials: None

Step 1: Ask the class to imagine that a terrible disaster has befallen everyone at the institution.

Step 2: Ask them to each write a letter in which they describe the event and how they responded. For example, they may write about a potential fire: "I ran out to the front door and turned left. I kept going straight ahead to the car park. I looked at the tree on fire. Then, I crossed the street so I could find someone to help and call 911."

---

33. *Just Imagine*

Type: Spelling / Grammar

Materials: Stamped envelopes

Step 1: Ask each student to write a letter in which they tell a wildly exaggerated story about themselves.

Step 2: Give them stamped envelopes. Have them mail the letters to you and enjoy reading them. These letters are usually hilarious and imaginative.

Step 3: During the next class, help students to correct spelling and grammar mistakes.

---

34. *Order Order!*

Type: Spelling

Materials: Soft toy mallet

Step 1: Divide the class into two teams. Have two volunteers sit at the front of the class back-to-back. Provide them with a random word.

Step 2: Students in each team must call out related words. They may not repeat words or hesitate for more than four seconds before saying the next related word.

Step 3: When the mallet moves over their heads, they must spell the word. If they spell it incorrectly, the mallet will touch them on the head. Call up two different students and continue until everyone has had a chance.

---

35.   *Chopstick Relay*

Type: Spelling

Materials: Markers

Step 1: Divide the students into groups of between five and ten. Hand each group a marker.

Step 2: Call out a word and have one student from each team come forward and write the first letter of the word on the board.

Step 3: When they return to their team, the next student should stand up and walk to the board and write the next letter. Do not allow anyone to stand up before their teammate has handed them the marker. No one should write more than one letter at a time. Points are deducted for doing so. The team who spells the most words correctly win.

---

36.   *Add A Word*

Type: Grammar / Spelling

Materials: None

Step 1: Split the class into two groups. In each group, let one student start a sentence with a word.

Step 2: The next one must say a word that continues the sentence. The word said by the next student in line must add to the sentence and make sense.

Step 3: Each student should have a go until the sentence is given a logical, grammatically correct end. The next student will then say "period" and start a new sentence.

If someone says a word that does not fit, one point for his team is forfeited. It may help to record the exercise and play it back for the class. Then errors can be identified and discussed.

Example:

Teacher: The topic is 'cooking.'

A: "My . . ."

B: ". . . wife"

C: ". . . has . . ."

D: ". . . metal . . ."

E: "... pots ..."

F: "... Period."

Step 4: The sentence could stop there. Ask the students why that sentence would be correct. The one who said "period" should be next to speak.

---

37.   *Common Letter*

Type: Spelling / Grammar

Materials: None

Step 1: Choose four or five nouns with the same initial letter. Write statements about the nouns or their definitions for students to see.

Step 2: In pairs, groups, or as a class have students guess what the original nouns were, and which initial letters the words have in common.

---

38.   *Spell It In The Past Tense*

Type: Spelling / Grammar

Materials: None

Step 1: Read a sentence to the class. Leave out only the verb.

Step 2: Ask the class to put the missing verb into past tense and spell it out.

---

39. *Call My Bluff*

Type: Spelling / Grammar

Materials: Dictionary or Picture dictionary

Step 1: Write an obscure word on the board and four definitions for it or four sentences containing it. Three should be wrong and the other correct. For example, with the word "angst" write out four "definitions" or four sentences containing the word. For example: 'To angst is a verb, the action of falling in love with someone'. In a sentence you could say "The boy angsted his best friend and she felt they could no longer be friends." And, "The angst of the patient drove the dentist from the room."

Step 2: The students must then read the definitions and decide whether they are true or false, or whether they are used correctly in the sentences or not.

This game can also be played in smaller groups of three or four. Each group will need its own dictionary.

Speaking and Pronunciation

40. *Village Fair*

Type: Speaking / Pronunciation

Materials: Miscellaneous items, monopoly money

Step 1: Each student picks something to sell at the market. They also decide what to buy there.

Step 2: Let the students walk around the class and sell, buy, and negotiate prices and quantities. Give them phrases with which they can start each sentence, such as:

"How about...?",

"Could you make that...?",

"That's a deal",

"No, I can't accept that…", etc.

Step 3: After 10 minutes, have the students report back to the class on their sales, purchases, remaining stock, and the money still in hand.

---

41. _Advice_

Type: Speaking / Pronunciation

Materials: None

Step 1: Put the students in a circle. Have one start by saying "I have a headache."

Step 2: The next should offer advice such as:

- "You should … + INFINITIVE."

- "You could try… + INFINITIVE."

- "If I were you, I would…"

- "Why don't you … + INFINITIVE?"

- "Have you thought about . . . (VERB)ING?"

Step 3: Give the students a variety of complaints or situations to which each should take a turn to offer advice.

---

42. _Prove It_

Type: Speaking / Pronunciation

Materials: None

Step 1: Give your students five statements to either prove or disprove. The statements must be in the form of a grammar structure learned in class. A statement may be like this: "Nobody in this class still lives with their parents."

Step 2: Students should speak to as many other students as possible so that they can either prove or disprove each statement.

Step 3: When they have asked around, they can feed back to the class.

Memory and Concentration

43.   *Months Of The Year*

Type: Memory / Concentration

Materials: Picture cards

Step 1: Assign picture cards to represent the months of the year, for example:

January - Fir tree

February - Heart

March - Wine glass

April - Shopping trolley

May - Flowers

June - Beach umbrella

July - Pen

August - Broken branch

September - Schoolbag

October - Pumpkin

November - Tax certificate

December - Christmas tree

Step 2: Have the students arrange the pictures correctly in the order of the months of the year.

---

44.   *Bingo With Irregular Verbs*

Type: Concentration / Memory

Materials: A 5x5 bingo grid with verbs

Step 1: Give each student a 5x5 grid containing 25 irregular verbs in the past tense. The grids for each student should be different.

Step 2: Call out sets of five verbs in their present tense until a student gets five verbs in a row, whether horizontally or diagonally. They should call out "Bingo!"

---

45.   *Concentration*

Type: Concentration / Memory

Materials: Projector, tablet, graphical interface / A 5x4 grid, cardboard squares and transparencies if using an overhead projector. (Make sure the squares are the same size as the blocks on the grid).

Step 1: Write the letter "T" at the top of the first column. Then, for each of the next four columns, write the letters "H", "I", "N", and "K". On the left side of the grid, number each row from 1 to 4.

Step 2: Think of ten pairs of items, such as opposites, irregular past tense forms, or pictures and their corresponding words. Put one word or picture in each space on the grid at random. Cover each space. If you are using an overhead projector, when you turn on the projector light, the students will see the grid, but each image or word will be dark.

Step 3: Get the students to pick two squares by naming the squares by their letter and number, such as "T4", "K2", or "N1". Uncover the spaces as each student calls out the squares. If the two spaces called match, write the student's name in the block. If the two spaces do not match, cover them back up and call on someone else to pick two blocks.

---

46. *Stop On A Word*

Type: Concentration

Materials: Music player

Step 1: Find a song with clear lyrics and seat students in a circle. Write a few words from the song's lyrics on the board.

Step 2: Play the song and let the students dance while you remove one chair from the circle. Pause the song very quickly when the singer sings a word on the board.

Step 3: When they hear the pause, each student must quickly find a seat and say which word they heard.

Step 4: If only one student remains standing at the end of the round, they get to answer revision questions related to the topic of the class. If more than one student remains standing, they can compete in a trivia question or another game to determine the winner.

---

47. *How Many Words?*

Type: Concentration / Memory

Materials: None

Step 1: Choose a sentence with several contractions, weak forms, and conjunctions. For example: "I'm going to go to the shop to see about buying fish." Say the sentence at normal speed.

Step 2: The students should count the number of words. Contractions count as two words. When the students give the correct answer, ask them to shorten what was said to a sentence with fewer words.

Turn-based Games

48. Snakes And Ladders Game

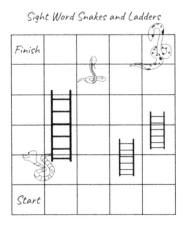

Sight Word Snakes and Ladders

Type: Turn-based

Materials: Snakes and Ladders board game, board, dice, and chips

Step 1: Fill the blocks on the game board with words, phrases, or pictures that you want the students to practice.

Step 2: Pair up the students and give each pair a game board, a die, and two chips.

Step 3: Students take turns rolling the die and move their chips forward according to the number the die lands on. Since each block contains a word or picture, the students must use them in a full sentence.

Step 4: If a student lands on a ladder, they move up the ladder, and if they land on the end of a snake, they must move back down. The first one to reach the end wins.

49.   *Name Six*

Type: Turn-based

Materials: 6 chairs in a circle, stuffed animals

Step 1: Choose one person to stand outside the circle and hand the stuffed animal to anyone inside the circle.

Step 2: The person outside the circle must say, "Name six…" and something that the person holding the toy should name six of. For example, the one inside the circle can name six 'animals with claws.'

Step 3: The person inside the circle should immediately pass the animal to the next student in the circle, and they have as long as it takes for the rest of the group to pass the animal around to finish naming the six things. All six things should be named before the animal is passed back to the person outside the circle.

Step 4: If the person outside the circle cannot name all six animals by the time the toy gets back to them, they have lost and must stand outside the group. They can then name something that the person in the circle now holding the stuffed animal should name six examples of. This will be more difficult now because the toy can only be passed between five people.

---

50.   *Air Write*

Type: Turn-based

Materials: None

Step 1: Pair up the students. Each partner takes a turn to 'write' a letter, number, word or shape in the air, and their partner should guess what it is.

This activity can be done as a group or as a whole class, and it helps if everyone gets a turn.

In another variation, the word or letter can be 'written' in the air backwards, and the others should guess what it is.

---

51.   *Four-letter Words*

Type: Turn-based

Materials: None

Step 1: Write a four-letter word on the board, for example, 'STAY.'

Step 2: In turns, students must make a new word from those letters by changing nothing but one letter at a time. The word 'STAY' could change to 'SLAY' and then to 'PLAY.'

Step 3: The game is more fun with the introduction of a time limit. Students score a point for each word they write, provided the words written must follow the rules and makes sense. The student who gets the most points within the given time wins.

---

52. *Mimes*

Type: Turn-based

Materials: Flashcards containing verbs

Each student takes a turn to get a flashcard with a verb on it. They must mime that action to the class and have them guess what they are doing. The other students may say, 'Are you swimming?' and the student with the flashcard may respond 'Yes, I am' or 'No, I am not.'

---

53. *Taboo*

Type: Turn-based

Materials: Flashcards

Step 1: Make flashcards with words on each like 'Home', 'Field', 'Company' etc.

Step 2: Below, in smaller font, write 4 or 5 keywords that are 'taboo' and cannot be used to describe the main word. For "home", the example could be 'kitchen', 'bedroom', 'family' etc.

Step 3: Any other words can be used to get teams to guess the main word on the card. Points are deducted in any of the taboo words are used.

---

54.   *Match Point*

Type: Turn-based

Materials: Flashcards of related verb-noun or adjective-noun pairs

Step 1: Put the cards up on the board in combination:

Cook – Pot

Browse — Internet

Sweep — Floor

Sit — Chair

Step 2: Introduce the cards as a set of verb-noun pairs.

Step 3: Shuffle the stack of verbs and the stack of nouns. Lay the sets face down in two rows.

Step 4: Let a student take a card from one set and another from the other set. With the two words they choose, have each student think up as many different sentences using those same two words as possible.

---

55.   *Stick-A-Card Guessing Game*

Type: Turn-based

Materials: Post-it notes

Step 1: Split the class into two groups. Call one student up to the front and stick a word on his back with a post-it note. Make sure all the other students can see it.

Step 2: Let the student standing in front ask the others as many questions as he needs to guess the word on his back. Deduct points from those guessing for (1) speaking another language, (2) gesturing, or (3) telling the student directly.

---

56.   *I Spy*

Type: Turn-based

Materials: Pen and paper and text excerpts

Step 1: The teacher can review vocabulary by choosing an item or picture in the class and saying, "I spy with my little eye something beginning with a L", for example.

Step 2: Then the students can walk around the room pointing out and asking about each item or picture whose name starts with an L.

---

57. *For Me To Know...*

Type: Turn-based

Materials: None

Step 1: One "knower" can be chosen, and the rest of the class should be "guessers".

Step 2: The knower should pick from 50 or so nouns on the board and choose to "be" that.

Step 3: The class may ask 20 questions to which the knower may only answer 'yes' or 'no'. The class must try to narrow down the options and guess what the "knower" has chosen from the board as soon as they are able to do so.

One-on-One Games

58. *Suppose That*

Type: One-on-one

Materials: None

Step 1: This game helps to improve fluency. The teacher can say: "Suppose that…" and create a scenario.

Step 2: The student should explain how they would respond in that situation.

The game could go like this:

"Suppose that you accidentally bump into someone you owe $25,000 to? What would you say to him?"

Step 3: Allow for response.

"Suppose that you discover that your car has been stolen from your driveway? What would you do?"

---

59. *Traffic Light Questions*

Type: One-on-one or team-based

Materials: Red, yellow, and green cards with six questions each on them

This game works well with adult students who are reluctant to speak about personal issues.

Step 1: Prepare three cards (a green, a yellow, and a red one) with six questions each. The six questions on the green card should be easy. The questions on the yellow card can be a little more difficult. The questions on the red card are personal.

Step 2: Have each student roll the die twice. The first roll picks the color of the card.

For example, 1 or 4 is for GREEN; 2 or 5 is for YELLOW; 3 or 6 is for RED.

Step 3: The second roll is to pick a question from the back of that card which the student should answer.

---

60.   *Twenty True Or False Items*

Type: One-on-one

Materials: Make a worksheet like the one below

Step 1: Make a list of twenty true or false thought-statements on a worksheet such as:

1. I never go to bed after midnight.

2. I have never stolen anything.

3. I study English for at least 2 hours each week.

4. I don't mind rain because there are still many things I can do.

5. I think motorbikes are dangerous.

6. Parents spoil their children nowadays.

7. The beach is only for relaxing and doing nothing.

8. I am an adventurous eater.

9. I would never use public transport.

10. Most people are good at heart.

11. I absolutely hate Mondays.

12. I would never raise my voice to someone older than me.

13. I think people who smoke are stupid.

14. People with large feet have more interesting personalities.

15. People who spend more than 2 hours a day on social media are wasting their time.

16. Spending more than $4,000 at a casino is a sin.

17. It is cruel to keep animals indoors.

18. I am intelligent.

19. I wish I knew karate.

20. I hate violence.

Step 2: Have each student write if the line is true or false in their case and one other sentence explaining why.

---

61.   *People Who...*

Type: One-on-one

Materials: A worksheet like this:

Step 1: Make a worksheet with prompts such as:

People who...

… park their cars on pavements...

… evade tax...

… litter…

… answer their cellphones in theatres…

Step 2: Let students complete the sentences realistically. They should not just be grammatically correct. In groups or as a class, students could take turns and call out their responses.

---

62.   *Personal Survey*

Type: One-on-one

Materials: A worksheet that looks like this:

Step 1: Make a list of personal questions on a worksheet such as:

PERSONAL SURVEY

1.   Did you have a happy childhood?

2.   When do you tell white lies? Give an example.

3.   Who is the most capable person in your country?

4.   Who is your favourite novelist?

5.   What has been your proudest moment?

6.   What was the worst moment of your life?

7.   Which song do you most hate now?

8.   Which was the last song you bought?

9.   Were you good at school?

10. Who has had the greatest influence on you?

11. What are you currently reading?

12. Where will you go when you die?

13. What do you admire most about yourself?

14. Which is your greatest fault?

15. Which is the last crime you committed?

16. What music would you like played at your funeral?

Step 2: Have the students respond to each question or have students interview each other. You could use this as a writing exercise.

---

63.   _My Town_

Type: One-on-one

Materials: None

Step 1: Ask the class: Do you like the town/city you live in? Why? Why not? Have them write down or call out their answers in turn.

Step 2: List all the positive and negative points the students mention and discuss any comments that are particularly interesting.

Step 3: Allow the students to compare their town/city with another one they know. By writing out full sentences they can contrast them in the following aspects:

• Pollution

• Traffic

• Nightlife

- Governance

- Planning

- City Parks

- Economy

Their sentences may start like this:

"My town is more polluted than X, because..."

"My city is wealthier than Y, because...:

Step 4: Finally, ask students to volunteer to tell the class which town/city is the best they have ever been to/seen? Why so?

Intermediate Level

The activities provided here are specifically targeted towards intermediate learners. The games are designed to help your students practice and improve their language skills, whether it be through speaking, reading, writing, or listening.

64.   *Make The Most Words*

Type: Warm-up

Materials: Marker pen

Step 1: Write a vocabulary item on the board based on a particular topic or idea.

Step 2: Put the students into groups of two or three and ask the students to create as many new words from it as they can.

You can also keep a score for each team on a point per word basis and give a bonus point for the longest word to keep the game competitive for the students.

---

65. *Expert Advice*

Type: Warm-up (also suitable for one-on-one instruction)

Materials: None

Step 1: Have students pair up and interview their partners about their hobbies and interests.

Step 2: After 2 minutes the pairs should switch. The format of this game is like speed dating.

---

66. *Make The Longest Words*

Type: Warm-up

Materials: Marker pen

Step 1: Write a topic word vertically down the board. The example provided below is "Fruits".

Step 2: Put the students into groups of two or three and ask them to think of the longest word that begins with each letter of the target word.

For example, for "Fruits", students might come up with:

"Fig"

"Raspberry"

"Ugli fruit"

"Tomato"

"Strawberry"

Step 3: You can keep score for each team on a point-per-word basis and give a bonus point for the longest word to keep the game competitive for the students.

---

67.   Conversation Starters

Type: Warm-up

Materials: None

Step 1: Write simple sentences on strips of paper. Each sentence should be a good conversation starter. As an example: "You look exotic in your red shoes," or "Would you like to meet my grandfather?" If the sentences are a little unusual, so much the better.

Step 2: Pair the students and give each pair a conversation starter. One should read the sentence aloud and the other should respond to it.

Step 3: When that conversation is over the other can read his conversation starter and have his partner respond.

68.   *What Does Your Name Mean?*

Type: Warm-up

Materials: Marker pen

Step 1: Ask your students to find and write down a fitting adjective that begins with the same letter as each letter of their first name.

You can allow students to use a dictionary or google if you want them to practice learning some new vocabulary. To make it more fun, ask them to use words that they feel describes them best, or their classmate.

For example:

Loving Uncompromising Cunning Young

---

69.   *Find Someone Who*

Type: Warm-up

Materials: Worksheet: "Find Someone Who…"

Step 1: Have students walk around the class with a worksheet that looks like this:

Find Someone Who:

	Name	Details
Speaks Spanish		
Uses English in their work		
Can play a musical instrument		
Lived in South America		
Likes to read story books		

Step 2: They should first brainstorm a good approach to start a conversation and draw out that sort of information. They should not ask the questions too directly.

Step 3: Have students share ideas on the kind of questions to ask to glean further details.

---

70.   *A to Z Board Race*

A	Banker	Chef
D	E	F
Gardener	H	I
J	K	L
M	N	O
Pilot	Q	Rockstar
S	T	U
V	Waiter	X
Y	Z	

Type: Warm-up

Materials: Marker pen

Step 1: Introduce the student to a theme. Then list the letters A to Z on the board.

Step 2: As a class, or in groups, students will call out or write a word relating to the topic for each letter of the alphabet.

---

71. *Odd One Out*

Type: Warm-up

Materials: Marker pen

Step 1: Make a short list of some items and ask the students to spot the odd one out.

Step 2: Then ask the students to come up with their own ideas and ask their classmates what they think the correct answer is. Some examples are as follows:

- Colosseum, Eiffel Tower, Big Ben, Angkor Wat – Angkor Wat is not in Europe.

- Helicopter, Horse & Carriage, Motorbike, Jet-Ski – Horse & Carriage is not motorized

---

Repetition and Drilling

72.   *Snakes & Ladders - Tenses*

Type: Drilling / Repetition

Materials: Snakes & Ladders Board game, die, chips, spinning game wheel with tenses

Step 1: On a game wheel, assign each segment to a tense. Place a verb on each block of the board game.

Step 2: The student who rolls the highest starts. They should roll again to move forward and spin the wheel.

Step 3: When a student lands on a verb he must make a sentence with that verb in the tense chosen on the wheel. If they fail, they must move back by the number rolled on the die.

---

73.   *Cards Of A Tense*

Type: Drilling / Repetition

Materials: Deck of cards

Assign each suit to a tense: Clubs, Diamonds, Spades and Hearts

Have students write out thirteen sentences for each of the cards from Ace to King.

In pairs, have a card drawn and the drawer must repeat the sentence in the tense of that suit. For example, if the card drawn is Ace of Spades the sentence would be the sentence they wrote for Ace in the tense of Spades.

---

74.   *Good Morning Balls*

Type: Repetition/Drilling

Materials: Three small, lightweight balls of different colors

Step 1: Assign a phrase to each ball.

Step 2: Have three students per group toss the balls between them. When they catch a ball, they should say the phrase assigned to that ball. For example:

Blue ball => "Good morning"

Orange ball => "How are you?"

Red ball => "Fine and you?"

---

75.   *Intonation Fun*

Type: Repetition

Materials: None

Step 1: Write down words on index cards and show them to the class. Have the students say the words with intonation changing depending on the intent. For instance:

"See you soon."

By a wife to a husband who is immigrating to work in another country.

By a prison warden to a prisoner just released.

By a school bully to a child on his first day of school.

By a music teacher waiting for her student to go in and play a music exam.

Step 2: Other words or phrases to practice intonation with may include:

"Hello"

"What are you doing here?"

"I don't think so."

"Why?"

"I do not get involved in politics."

"We need to talk."

With a more advanced class, you can have them suggest different intentions underlying the words.

Team-based Games

76. _Where Shall I Go?_

Type: Team-based

Materials: Furniture

Step 1: Arrange a maze (this can be done with furniture inside or outside the classroom).

Step 2: When the class arrives, keep them outside the maze area until they are paired.

Step 3: Give each pair a blindfold so that one should be blindfolded, and the other should give directions through the maze.

---

77. *Word Jumble Race*

Type: Grammar / Spelling

Materials: Hat, five pages of different colors

Step 1: Have five sentences written out on five different color pages - one sentence to one color.

Step 2: Cut the sentences up into words and phrases.

Step 3: Assign the class to groups of about four and give each group a hat with the colored slips of paper.

Step 4: Have them arrange the words and phrases into five correct sentences. The first team to arrange the phrases correctly wins.

---

78. *Getting To Know You*

Type: Team-based

Materials: None

Step 1: Give each student an index card and have them pair up. Give them six questions to ask each other, such as:

- Where were you born?

- What is your favorite food?

- What kind of work do you do?

- What do your parents do?

- What is your favorite book?

- What are your hobbies?

Step 2: Students should write down the answers given by their partners and then switch partners.

Step 3: Once they are done, students may be given the opportunity to share what they have learned about their classmates with the rest of the class.

---

79.   *Active Brainstorming*

Type: Team-based

Materials: Markers

Step 1: Divide the class into no more than four groups and write a topic on the board. Designate writing space on the board to each of the groups.

Step 2: Each group should choose one writer who will go to the front and write down the words related to the topic that their team members yell at them. With most of the class yelling, this game might get a little boisterous.

Step 3: Change writers every 60 seconds so that everyone in the class has a chance to write on the board.

Step 4: Pause the game, check the entries, and provide a new topic after three or four minutes of writing.

---

80.   *The Recruiter*

Type: Team-based

Materials: None

Step 1: Assign students to groups of at least five. One should be chosen to be the "hotel owner", who must appoint a "restaurant manager".

Step 2: Provide the "hotel owner" buttons of three different colors, such as red, yellow, and green. The other team members should come in one by one for an interview.

Step 3: Based on the results of the interview, each should receive a button from the "hotel owner". A red button could be given to the worst candidate for the job, while a yellow button goes to each inappropriate candidate, and a green button to the most promising candidate for the job.

Step 4: The "hotel owner" should call the team together and explain the personality traits they require in the "restaurant manager".

Index cards with adjectives describing personalities will help students to extend their vocabularies. It may also help to rotate recruiters and candidates within the group, as well as the positions they are recruiting for.

---

81.   Two-step Quiz

Type: Team-based

Materials: Word Up question sheets

Step 1: Pick a topic. The topic may be a series, reality shows, cities, animals, or even members of the class. Someone must choose something in that category. For example, in the category of "this class," the student might silently think of "Julio." The class can ask no more than twenty questions to narrow down and identify Julio. The students might ask questions like "Does this person use makeup?" or "Does this person speak Spanish?"

The team who wins in step one can earn bonus points for correctly answering a question from a 'Word up' question sheet. Make sure the 'Word Up' sheets are pitched at the correct level for your class.

Step 2: This step is played after a team wins step one. This team earns one point for winning step one and the chance to earn a bonus point by correctly answering a 'Word Up' question. If a wrong answer is given in step two, one point is deducted. The team may choose not to play for a bonus point. The first team to score four points wins and ends the game.

---

82.   Match Of The Day

Type: Team-based

Materials: 'Word Up' question sheet

This game is similar to the 'Two-step Quiz'. It might work with a class who share an interest in the same sport. In this example, we will use UEFA League football.

Step 1: Get two groups of three students to bring their chairs to the front and face each other. Draw a scorecard on the board that looks like this:

| Teams | 1st half | 2nd half |
Final Score

How to play

Step 2: Name each of the teams in front after a UEFA club. Ask for a student to volunteer as the 'referee'. The referee should use the 'Word Up' question and answer sheets, write the team's names, and keep the score on the board. The teacher can act as the timekeeper.

Step 3: Teams are given fifteen minutes to play against each other, answering all the questions from the 'Word up' question sheet. If the scores are tied, a penalty shootout may be needed.

Step 4: When the time is up, call a spectator up from the audience and ask him to write down on a piece of paper the name of either a club or player he knows a lot about. The teams may ask the spectator, 'Is it a club or a player?' Then the referee tosses a coin to decide the team that kicks off. He gets the teams to take turns asking the spectator questions about the club or player. After each question, the team must guess. If they fail to guess correctly, the next team goes. If the spectator is unsure of the answer, the team can ask another question.

Step 5: When a team guesses correctly, they win, and the scores are updated. Next, name another team and call them to the 'stadium.' Begin with the 'Word Up' question sheet again.

---

83.   *Liar Liar*

Type: Team-based

Materials: None

Step 1: In groups of three, let two students ask the other one five questions. Examples of the questions could be as below. The student must answer each question with the words 'Yes, of course.' This will not always be true, but the purpose of the game is to get students to probe further by asking other questions and determining which stories are true and which are not.

Have you ever

- been on a film set?

- danced on a table at a restaurant?

- gone bungee jumping?

- climbed to the summit of a very high mountain?

- chased a criminal?

Step 2: The student should answer "Yes, of course" to each of the questions and then should be cross-examined by the other two to determine if they are telling the truth. When the other two have reached a decision, they should mark their verdicts 'true' or 'false' on the question page.

84. *Present Continuous Videos*

Type: Team-based

Materials: Video with action and no dialogue (*Mr. Bean* episodes are ideal)

Step 1: Pair students. Have one actor and one watcher. The watcher may see the video playing and describe to the actor what to do, without making any gestures. The actor must listen and do exactly as described by the watcher.

Step 2: The winning partnership has the actor performs most like the character on screen.

---

85. *Whisper Circles*

Type: Team-based

Materials: None

Step 1: Put students into groups of no more than ten each. Each group should form a circle.

Step 2: Pick a group leader from each group and ask them to read a message from an index card. They should whisper the message in the ear of a teammate.

Step 3: That teammate must whisper the exact same message in the same words to the person sitting next to them and so the message must go around.

Step 4: When the last person in the circle hears the message, they should write down what he heard. The first team to write the message in the same words as are on the original index card wins.

---

86.   *Match And Catch The Riddle*

Type: Team-based

Materials: None

Step 1: Pair students. Each pair must have a questioner and an answerer. Have the questioners make up a riddle. The riddles can be bizarre or funny.

Step 2: The answerer must come up with an answer. A riddle like this would be acceptable:

"How can you tell the difference between cake mix and corn flour?" The answerer's response may be: "Read the label." Or perhaps, "Why is mayonnaise not being served?" The answer is "because it is just dressing."

For lower levels, you may need to write the riddles and their answers out. Hand either a riddle or its answer to each student and allow students to pair up on that basis.

---

87.   *Crazy Story*

Type: Team-based

Materials: None

Step 1: In rows, hand each student on the end a sheet of paper. Have them write the answer to the question "Who?" by providing a man's name and a little detail about him.

Step 2: The students should fold the page over the line to hide what they wrote and hand the page to the person next to them. The next student must answer the question "What did he do?" They should also fold the page to cover just the line that they wrote.

Step 3: The student who gets the page next must write the answer to the question "To whom did he do it?" and the next question is "Where was it done?" Fold the page and hand it over. The next in line should answer "What did he say?" Then ask, "How did she respond?" Write what happened next, and finally, write down "Where are they now?"

At lower levels, you may need to write the format of the story on the board:

..........., (man's name) was a ……..…….. (description)

He …………………………….. (action)

to ……………., who………….. (woman's name, description)

in/at ....(place)

He said ....

And she responded by ....

Next, ...

Now he is ....

and she ....

Check the stories for errors of spelling and grammar.

---

88.   *Find The Differences*

Type: Team-based (Also suitable for one-on-one instruction)

Materials: None

Step 1: Hand each pair in the class two almost identical pictures. No partners are allowed to see each other's pictures.

Step 2: They must describe the pictures to each other and identify the differences.

Step 3: The first pair to correctly identify all the differences wins. They are allowed to ask each other any questions and describe the pictures in detail, but they may not look at the other's picture.

---

89.   *Enigma*

Type: Team-based (Also suitable for one-on-one instruction)

Materials: None

Step 1: Hand students a message written in code and tell them to decipher it. Tell them the first word, as a clue, is "the".

Step 2: When they are finished deciphering the message, ask them to send an encrypted message to a classmate. Some may want to create a new code. This exercise can really help to correct and improve spelling and even grammar. An example of a message could be:

"The submarine will emerge at midnight."

"If you would like to meet"

"Please take the thirty-nine steps"

"Down from the castle gate to the wharf."

The entire message should be presented alone, with no accompanying key, like this:

"If you would like to meet, please take the thirty-nine steps down from the castle gate to the wharf."

---

90. *Mastermind*

Type: Team-based

Materials: Mastermind question cards

Step 1: Print out questions for a game of Mastermind. The questions should be in four categories: "Geography", "Science", "Music", and "Sports".

Step 2: Create a stage area where three contestants will sit.

Step 3: Act as quiz master and have the first contestant choose a category. Put one question to one student at a time in each round.

Step 4: If the first student asked is unable to answer, the 'audience', that is, any of the rest of the class, may answer. At the end of five rounds, the contestant with the most correct answers wins.

---

91.   *Team Quiz*

Type: Team-based

Materials: None

Step 1: Prepare a worksheet with at least 20 sentences but leave out only one word in each sentence.

Step 2: Put a scorecard on the board to keep track. Decide how many points will be needed to end the game. Ten points are usually adequate.

Step 3: Ask one team at a time to identify the missing word. The team member who puts his hand up first may answer. If he is wrong, allow the other team 15 seconds to answer correctly. If they fail to, no points are scored. Continue until the score of ten is reached by either team.

You may want to ask a student to be the quiz master. This will free you to focus on correcting pronunciation.

---

92. _Quiz Show_

Type: Team-based

Materials: Trivial Pursuit Junior, Mastermind or Word Up question cards

Step 1: Use question cards or question-and-answer sheets appropriate for the level of your class.

Step 2: Assign a quizmaster and have contestants write their answers down. The quizmaster should be timed and should read all the questions within approximately three minutes.

Step 3: At the end, the number of correct answers, less any words misspelled, will equal the contestant's score.

For a variation, the entire class can play this game at the same time.

---

93. _Heads or Tails_

Type: Team-based

Materials: Word Up question sheets, coins

Step 1: Use two 'Word up' question sheets, printed front and back. Two question sheets from Level 2 and two from Level 4 or 5. Give one copy to each pair in the class. Hand each pair a coin. Students should draw a scoring table like this:

(Student's name)	Game 1	Game 2	Game 3
Missing Word			
Crossword Clues			
Multiple Choice			
Spelling			

Step 2: One student should ask lower-level questions and the other student should ask higher-level questions from one side of the worksheet. A coin toss will decide who plays first. The coin is tossed again to pick the level at which the first category's questions should be answered.

Step 3: When all those questions have been answered, the coin is tossed again to decide at which level the next category's questions should be answered. The play continues until all the questions have been answered.

94. *Spelling Review*

Type: Spelling

Materials: None

Step 1: Help the students to spell correctly by writing cryptic messages on the board that would be easy to decipher. For example:

URAQT => You are a cutie.

ICURYY4me => I see you are too wise for me.

CU@8 => See you at eight.

Etc.

---

95. *Pronunciation Bingo*

Type: Spelling

Materials: None

Step 1: Have two students sit in the front with their backs to one another and give them a sentence but leave out one word such as the words in the list below.

Step 2: After you have read the sentence, repeat two possible pronunciations of the word, and have the students put their hands up when they hear the pronunciation, they think is right. Words might include the following:

pro'-gress OR pro-gre'ss

pre'-sent OR pre-se'nt

pro'-test OR pro-te'st

con'-tract OR con-tra'ct

de'-sert OR de-se'rt

re'-bel OR re-be'l

sus'-pect OR sus-pe'ct

con'-flict OR con-fli'ct

re'-cord OR re-co'rd

con'-vict OR con-vi'ct

etc.

You can have the other students write down the words and underline the correct syllable to be stressed at the same time.

---

96.   *Slogan Goodbye*

Type: Spelling/Grammar

Materials: Clothing markers

Step 1: Students can say goodbye to each other at the end of a semester with a commemorative T-shirt.

Step 2: Ask each student to write a message to their classmates on their T-shirt, such as a blessing, proverb or, slogan they particularly like.

---

97. *Spelling Competition*

Type: Spelling

Materials: None

Step 1: Team the students up. Have each team appoint a writer. Give them a word to write on the board by asking a question such as:

"Which language is spoken in the Congo?"

Have the writers rush to the board to write "French".

"Which precious metal begins with a P?"

And the next writer from each team can write "Platinum".

Step 2: The teams who have spelled the most words correctly win.

---

98. *Bingo*

Type: Spelling

Materials: Blank Bingo grid

Step 1: Instead of filling in the bingo grids yourself, have your students do it. Prepare review questions from the textbook and trivia that your students would most likely know. Each question should cover the grammar that has been studied before. The answers should be only one word.

Step 2: Hand each student a blank bingo grid. Start by asking them to fill in the grid with the answers to each question. When they have completed that exercise, start the bingo game.

Step 3: Read new questions for which the answer is one of the sentences formed in a correctly answered row on a Bingo grid. If the full sentence is on someone's Bingo grid, they may yell "Bingo". Then, toss them a prize.

This game can be played to test grammar, vocabulary, tenses, and many other aspects of language.

---

99. _Contractions_

Type: Spelling

Materials: Print out cards with contractions and their longer forms

Step 1: Cards should be printed in pairs and not together:

would've (would have)

couldn't have (could not have)

oughtn't to (ought not to)

shan't (shall not)

Step 2: This game could suit intermediate level English speakers well if they are asked to write down the contraction or the longer form correctly after having the index cards flashed at them. They can then make a sentence with the words

---

100. *Target*

Type: Spelling

Materials: None

Step 1: Write a nine-letter word on the board and get each student to write down all the smaller words that can be made using the same letters.

Step 2: Set a target of words to find. For the words below a fair target might be 50 words. Acronyms are not allowed.

For example:

REPLICATE

reap, lit, pile, clip, trap, rape, place, plait, plea etc.

GREYHOUND

dough, hour, huge, nudge, rogue, rude, undergo, young etc.

Step 3: Then check for spelling and let students add the words to their vocabularies.

Turn-based Games

101. *The Mime*

Type: Turn-based

Materials: Hat

Step 1: Put a few cards with scenarios on them into a hat. Have each student in turn come to the front and mime the scenario on the card they draw for the class to guess.

The scenarios can be simple like:

Drive through a hailstorm

Wash the dishes on a ship during a storm

Points can be awarded to the first one in the class to guess correctly.

Step 2: Give the students a chance to write out the scenarios and pass a scenario across to someone in their row. At random, call students up to mime their scenario. All students must mime at least one scenario.

Step 3: After the student has mimed the scenario and the class has guessed correctly, ask the student to spell a specific word related to the scenario. For example, if the scenario is "Drive through a hailstorm," you could ask the student to spell "windshield wipers" or "sleet." This adds a spelling challenge to the game and helps reinforce vocabulary related to the scenario.

---

102. *Extreme Times*

Type: Turn-based

Materials: None

Step 1: Sketch a scenario and have each group discuss how they would react. For example, to groups of three or four you might say:

"Imagine you are on a deserted island with a group of friends. You have limited supplies and need to make some difficult decisions in order to survive. There is only one raft available, and it can only carry four people. You must choose which three individuals to take with you. The people on the island are:

- Your best friend who is very strong and athletic.
- A young child who is sick and needs medical attention.
- An elderly person who is frail and may not be able to handle the physical demands of the journey.
- A person with a fear of water who may struggle to swim to safety.
- A person who is very smart but not very physically fit.
- A person who is very skilled at building things but may not be very good at navigation."

Step 2: Other scenarios may be like this:

"You find a wallet containing $25,000 and the owner's driver's license. That is exactly the money you owe on your child's medical treatment. Without that operation, your child will not survive. What would you do with the money?"

Step 3: Create other extreme situations and test your students' comprehension, conversation skills, and preconceptions.

---

103. *Tell Me Why*

Type: Turn-based

Materials: None

Step 1: Test students' conversation skills, comprehension, and logic with the question "Why?"

Here are some examples:

Why do people nod when they agree?

Why are plants green but the sky is blue?

Why do brides wear white, but bridegrooms wear black?

Why is glass made of sand?

---

104. *If You Were . . .*

Type: Turn-based

Materials: None

Step 1: Have one student chosen to leave the room. From amongst those still in the room, choose someone else. The class should discuss that person, saying something like this:

"If this person were a fruit, which fruit would they be?" (It could be a car, flower, tree, animal, food, or drink.) All the students can work together to decide, and each suggestion should be correctly formed. Suggestions should be made in a full, correct sentence. For example: "If they were an animal, they would be a mongoose."

Step 2: When the class has decided, the student who left the room can return and ask about the qualities of the animal, fruit, or other category chosen. They will need to guess who was chosen by the class. Then the game can be repeated with another student leaving the room.

105. *Hot Topics*

Type: Turn-based

Materials: Index cards

Step 1: Write topics on index cards such as:

- Love

- Violence,

- The Supernatural,

- Death Penalty,

- Cloning,

- War,

- Colonizing Mars,

- The Robot Workforce

Step 2: Give each student a turn to speak for a minute on the topic. Do not show them the card until just before their one-minute speech begins. They should present their opinion on the topic to the class.

For example: "It is amazing that people can clone animals. However, I do not want to eat meat from a cloned animal. Many are very poor, and they might be willing to eat anything. I do not think it is good to clone everything. For instance, cloning humans could have serious ethical implications."

106. *Matching Cards 1 - Opposites*

Type: Turn-based

Materials: Print out cards with opposites on them to be paired

Step 1: Divide the class into groups of three or four. Give a complete set of 18 cards to each pair.

Step 2: Have them lay the cards face down in grids of 3x6. One player may turn two cards over and show them to the group.

Step 3: If those two are a matching pair of opposites, for example, "proof" and "refutation" or "tall" and "short," the player may keep the cards. If they are not a match, they should put the cards back in their places, and the next player should take their turn. When all the cards are claimed as matches, the student sitting with the most correctly matched pairs wins.

This game tests short-term memory and vocabulary. Students try to remember the cards they have seen.

Variation: Before a student may keep a pair of matching cards, they must use the words in a correct sentence.

---

107. *Matching Cards 2 - Phrasal Verbs*

Type: Turn-based

Materials: Print out cards with phrasal verbs and synonyms to be matched

Step 1: Divide the class into groups of four. Give each group a set of 18 cards to lay down in a 3x6 grid.

Step 2: The first player starts by opening any two cards. If they think that the verbs mean the same thing, they may keep both cards. If the two cards do not match, they will be placed face down again exactly as they were. A correct match is worth 5 points.

Step 3: If the player doubts, they can ask the teacher to confirm and lose 3 points.

Step 4: At the end of the game, the player with the highest score wins. If any player has unmatched cards remaining, they will lose six points from their total score.

---

108.   *Charades*

Type: Turn-based

Materials: Index cards with compound nouns or phrasal verbs

Step 1: Players take turns miming each word on the card. For instance, if the card says 'Bookkeeper', the player would mime until the class correctly guesses 'book'.

Step 2: Then, they would continue miming so that the class would guess 'keeper'.

Step 3: Someone in the class must say 'bookkeeper' before the miming player's turn ends.

Step 4: The miming player may only nod when someone calls out the correct word.

A similar game can be played using phrasal verbs such as 'keep swimming' and 'double park'.

109. *What's The Proverb?*

Type: Turn-based

Materials: None

Step 1: Have a student take their turn to mime the keywords in proverb. They may show with their fingers how many words are in the proverb. For example, if they want to mime "a stitch in time saves nine" they would hold up six fingers. They might point to the second finger and mime a stitching or sewing action. Then, they could show the fourth finger and point at their wrist to indicate time.

Step 2: They would continue until the class guesses and suggests the word 'time'.

Step 3: After the class has correctly guessed the word, the player should continue until someone recognizes the complete proverb and shares it with everyone.

---

110. *The Music Club*

Type: Turn-based (Also suitable for one-on-one instruction)

Materials: Music player

Step 1: Pick a theme, such as "Myths we believe as children" or "How the world has changed".

Step 2: Have each student bring a song to class that they connect with that theme. Each one should play his song for the class and explain why that song was chosen and how it connects to the theme of the game.

Step 3: The others may ask questions about the history and meaning of the song.

---

111. *Anecdote*

Type: Turn-based (Also suitable for one-on-one instruction)

Materials: None

Step 1: Each student has a turn to share a true story of something that happened to them, recently or in the more distant past. They should sketch the scene and begin to tell the story and stops short of the end.

Step 2: They ask the other students to guess what happened next.

---

112. *Password*

Type: Turn-based

Materials: None

Step 1: Select one student to leave the room while the others choose a password to allow them back into the class.

Step 2: When the student returns, the class can ask questions to prompt them to say the password and rejoin the lesson.

Step 3: The student must answer all questions truthfully and will lose a point for revealing the password. For example:

Teacher: "A, please step outside." (Exit A)

B: "Can we use 'mustard' as the password?"

All: "Agreed."

Teacher: "A, you may come back in."

C: "Which condiment might you add to fries?"

A: "Ketchup."

D: "What color is Daniel's shirt?"

A: "Yellow."

At this point, A should guess that the password is 'mustard'.

---

113.   *WikiHow*

Type: Turn-based (Also suitable for one-on-one instruction)

Materials: None

Assign students the task of demonstrating how to do something to the class. Before the exercise begins, hand out slips of paper with the assigned actions. Examples of actions may include:

- How to hot-wire a car

- How to make leather

- How to find water in the desert

- How to make a tiramisu

- How to change a door lock

This can be as simple or as complicated as necessary. It can be presented as a 2-minute infomercial without any props. Encourage them to be creative and engaging in their presentation.

---

114.   *Give A Speech*

Type: Turn-based (Also suitable for one-on-one instruction)

Materials: None

Step 1: Teach students how to speak persuasively. Choose a controversial statement such as "Nuclear energy is green and safe", "Robots cannot replace our workforce", "Colonizing Mars is not a viable solution", "Religion should be prohibited globally", "Cultured meat can end world hunger", or any other controversial topic. Provide an outline to be delivered as a 10-minute speech to persuade the group of your viewpoint on this.

Step 2: Assume that some members of your audience disagree with you and aim to help them understand your perspective. Your goal is to change people's minds, and your body language, voice, and logic will play a crucial role.

Explain to students that their presentations will be judged based on the following criteria:

Body language: Confidence, poise, natural gestures, and correct posture.

Articulation: Clear, unmuffled speech with correctly formed vowel sounds.

Pronunciation: Avoidance of slang and word whiskers, and correctly formed consonant sounds.

Pitch: Appropriate intonation and modulation.

Speed: Keeping a steady but unhurried pace while efficiently varying the speed.

Pausing: Effective use of pauses to emphasize ideas and move on to a new point.

Volume: Maintaining adequate volume for all in the room to hear without sounding aggressive or shy.

Logic: Leading listeners from a well-known premise to a reasonable conclusion backed up by three main arguments that are clear, concise, and direct.

Reasonableness: Acknowledging opposing ideas and presenting your case as the conclusion of those well-informed on the subject without making strong assertions with no evidence to back them.

Interest arousing: Motivating your listeners and stirring their emotions with an illustration or analogy that makes your main point stand out and resonates with the audience

Step 3: Encourage students to prepare and practice their speeches thoroughly, paying attention to these criteria to make their presentations persuasive and effective.

---

115. *That's My Job*

Type: Turn-based

Materials: None

Step 1: Have a student pick an occupation, and then have the others ask no more than 20 questions to decide which occupation it is. The student may not answer any question with more than yes or no.

For example, if the subject is "occupations," then the questions might go like this:

Do you work in the evenings?

Must you work with a team?

Do you work outside?

Do you use time sheets?

Step 2: When the student's occupation is identified, another one may take a turn.

Concentration and Memory

116. *Remember and Tell*

Type: Concentration / Memory

Materials: None

Step 1: Have the class divide into groups and form circles of no less than six students each. Start one in the circle off with a story like, "Once, there was a young man."

Step 2: The next student in the circle should repeat that line and add one more line to it, such as, "Once, there was a young man who lived in a very tall building in town."

Step 3: The next one in the circle would then repeat what the previous two said and add one more line to the story.

This game tests students' memory and creativity as the story is developed.

One-on-One Games

117. _Kryptonian_

Type: One-on-One

Materials: None

Introduce yourself as an extraterrestrial life form inhabiting a human body to study intelligent life on Earth. Ask questions about anything and everything in the room. The conversation may go like this:

K: What is this?

A: It's a book.

K: What's a "book"?

A: A book is a collection of written or printed pages bound together, containing information or entertainment.

K: What does "entertainment"?

A: Entertainment refers to activities that provide amusement or enjoyment.

K: Can you give me an example?

A: Sure, watching movies, playing games, or reading books can be considered entertainment.

Move around and enquire about several objects in the room.

118. *Listening Exercise (Song Puzzle)*

Type: One-on-one

Materials: Music player, songs, lyric sheets

Print out a copy of song lyrics for each student in the class. Cut out each line separately and jumble the strips of paper. Play the song for the students and have them arrange the lines in the order in which they are sung in the song. The first to complete all the lyrics correctly wins. It may be necessary to replay the song several times.

---

119. *Write A Story*

Type: One-on-One

Materials: Projector; Wacom tablet or graphic interface

Step 1: On a projector, display a scene of a location such as a small village street, a mountainside, a farmer's field, etc. Ask each student to write down their ideas about the place and predict what may happen there.

Step 2: Introduce a character to the scene and ask students to incorporate that character into their stories. Repeat the process by adding additional characters and challenging students to incorporate them into their stories to build the plot. Keep adding new characters and ask students to complete their stories with an exciting climax and a satisfying resolution.

Step 3: Finally, pass the stories around the class for others to read and enjoy. Remind the students to spellcheck their work before submitting it.

---

120.   *Plan The Essay*

Type: One-on-one

Materials: None

Step 1: Pick a topic and hand each student a large piece of paper. They must write down "What," "Where," "When," "Who," "Why," and "How" on the sheet. Then they must brainstorm ideas and jot them down around each of those main question words.

Step 2: Have the students break the points they have brainstormed into an introduction, body, and conclusion. Let them turn the sheet over and jot down the outline of their essay in point form.

Step 3: Review the outline's logic as a class, and then allow students to begin writing their essays.

---

121. *Animals, Our Friends*

Type: One-on-one

Materials: None

Step 1: Read a story to the students about an animal rescuing a human. An example of such a story may go like this:

"In the summer of 2014, a man from Armenia fell under a truck he was repairing. His leg got caught beneath the wheel. The area was deserted, and no one heard his cries for help. However, a crow heard and mimicked his cries. Someone heard the crow calling from a nearby campsite and alerted the patrol guards. The guards came and reversed the car, freeing them injured man who sustained only minor injuries."

Step 2: Then ask the students questions such as:

1. Have you ever been in a similar situation?

2. Has an animal ever helped you in some way?

3. Do you think humans need animals, and why?

4. List the most helpful animals you know of. What makes them helpful?

5. List the difficulties associated with having animals around.

6. When you see a spider, fly, mosquito, moth, or other creature in your house, what is your first reaction? Why?

122.   *Rank Your Conversation Style*

Type: One-on-one

Materials: None

Step 1: Ask the students to respond to the following statements with a 'yes' or a 'no'. Award one point for 'yes' and two points for 'no'.

In conversations with people, I:

• Tend to be blunt

• Tend to criticize others

• Can be sarcastic

• Ask many questions to better understand people's thoughts

• Dislike admitting when I'm wrong

• Maintain eye contact and use gestures freely

• Generalize

• Freely and genuinely compliment people

• Use profanity

• Prefer talking about myself

• Truly listen to others

• Prefer discussing topics such as history, economics, or technology over personal issues

• Enjoy discussing people's problems, hopes, and challenges

• Feel more comfortable expressing myself through writing than in face-to-face conversations

• Prefer straightforward, yes-or-no answers to questions

Step 2: Have the students tally up their scores and rank their conversation type:

15-20 points: You're a conversation superstar!

10-14 points: You're on the right track, keep practicing and refining your skills.

5-9 points: You may need to work on your communication skills a bit more.

0-4 points: Don't worry, everyone starts somewhere!

---

123. *Rate The Gadget*

Type: One-on-one

Materials: None

Step 1: We may feel that our refrigerators, washing machines, kettles, cellphones, lights, and ovens are essential to life. They do save time. But which of them are really necessary? And, if we had to do without any of them, what could we do instead that would serve the same purpose? Which of these machines is most important? Which is least important?

Step 2: Fill in an importance rating from 1 - 10 and next to each item write down what you would use instead if you had to do without it.

____ Refrigerator

____ Washing machine

____ Shower

___ Toilet

___ Coffee machine

___ TV

___ Radio

___ Cellphone

___ Light bulb

___ Oven

---

124. _Do We Need It?_

Type: One-on-one

Materials: None

Step 1: Perfume, hair dryers, beautiful dinnerware, wine glasses and good furniture are nice to have. Ask the students to rate these items in order of their value to improving quality of life:

___Perfume

___Hair styling tools

___Mirrors

___Apple Watch

___Hip flasks

___Special wine glasses

___Cellphones

___Curtains

___Expensive furniture

___Tablets

Step 2: Ask the students to explain the reasons behind their ratings. The purpose of the exercise is to practice conversation and offer sound reasons for the ratings given.

---

125. *To Spend Time*

Type: One-on-one

Materials: None

Step 1: Practice conversation by asking questions about how students prefer to spend their time. The questions may go like this:

1. When are you most likely to check social media?

2. What do you watch on television?

3. What do you usually do during commercial breaks?

Step 2: Make a list of the most common responses. Some examples may be:

- I message friends

- I read whatever is lying around

- I look inside the refrigerator

- I change channels

- I look for something else to do

4. Which ways do you prefer to pass the time/occupy your mind when you are:

- Waiting in a queue?

- Waiting for a date?

- Sitting in the auditorium before a show begins?

- Stuck in a traffic jam?

- Getting my hair done in the salon?

Step 3: Feel free to add more questions or scenarios that you find interesting or relevant. The purpose of this exercise is to practice conversation and learn about each other's preferences and habits.

---

126.   *Tell Me About Myself*

Type: One-on-one

Materials: None

Step 1: On the board, draw pictures, symbols, numbers, words, and anything else except sentences which describe you. You might include information such as your date of birth, the number of children or siblings you have, trees, or whether you come from a forested area, and so on.

Step 2: As you draw, have the others describe you based on what you have written on the board.

Step 3: Give the students an opportunity to do the same exercise and have a partner describe them.

---

127. *Missing Headlines*

Type: One-on-one

Materials: Newsprint

Step 1: Print news pages out from the web and cut the stories out. Keep the headlines separate.

Step 2: Ask students to match stories with their headlines.

128. *Quick Quiz*

Type: One-on-one

Materials: Word Up question sheet

Step 1: Use only the front of a "Word Up" question sheet. Keep the sheet faced down until the starting bell.

Step 2: Then, let students work alone or in pairs to complete the questions in a set time limit, perhaps ten minutes. Let them write as many answers as they can think of for each question in any order they choose.

Step 3: After the time is up, check who got the correct answers. If no one answered correctly, tell students what the answer was.

Step 4: Score their answers, and the pair with the highest score wins.

Advanced Level

This section offers a variety of elaborate games that are suited to the needs of advanced learners. These activities are intended to be intriguing and thought-provoking, encouraging students to use and expand their knowledge of the language in complex and nuanced ways. Whether it's through debating, interpreting complex texts, or analyzing spoken language, these games offer a stimulating and rewarding way for advanced learners to improve their English proficiency.

129. *Mixed Up Sentence (Anagram version)*

Type: Warm-up

Materials: Marker pen

Step 1: Write a sentence on the board and ask the students to unscramble each word of the sentence. For example:

Thaw era uoy giogn ot od otayd?

What are you going to do today?

---

130. *What Do You Know About Cars?*

Type: Warm-up

Materials: Marker pen

Step 1: Put the students into groups and ask them to write down as many facts as they can about a particular topic (cars, countries, mountains, etc.).

Step 2: Give students a point for every correct sentence they can come up with.

131.   *Think Of Ten*

Type: Warm-up

Materials: Marker pen

Step 1: Choose a certain criterion or topic, and ask students to create a list of 10 things relating to the said criterion/topic. For example:

- Sports that are played with a racket

- Cities that begin with the letter B

- Presidents of the USA

---

132.   *The Gossip*

Type: Warm-up

Materials: None

Step 1: Have the entire class sit in a circle. Whisper a full story into the ear of a student. Have the student repeat the story to the person next to them in a low whisper.

Step 2: Each student must listen to the story and pass it on to the person next to them.

Step 3: When the last person hears the story, they should tell it out to the class.

Step 4: Usually, many additions to and subtractions from the story have been made. Allow the students to share how the final version of the story differs from the version they heard. Alternatively, show a student a written story and ask them to whisper it to the next student in line.

---

133. *Things To Do With An Apple*

Type: Warm-up

Materials: Marker pen, apple

Step 1: If possible, bring an apple (or some other prop) and present the students with the concept of an apple.

Step 2: Split the students into groups and ask them to list as many unusual uses for the apple as they can. For example, a weapon, stationary holder, fashion accessory.

The team with the most ideas win.

---

134. *Circle Game*

Type: Warm-up (Concentration)

Materials: Chairs

Step 1: This game is great for listening. Arrange chairs in the classroom so that everyone is sitting in a circle.

Step 2: Assign each person a seat with a number. Instruct them, for example:

- "Everyone who has a younger brother, change seats"

- "If you have lived in your current home for less than one year, change seats"

- "If you own a pair of red trousers, change seats"

Only those who fit the description should change seats.

Step 3: With each instruction, one seat should be removed. The last one on a seat, wins.

---

135. *Flyswatters Game*

Type: Warm-up

Materials: Index cards, colored cardboard "flies", flyswatters

Step 1: Divide the class into teams and assign a different color to each team. Place index cards with the words from a passage around the classroom and place one cardboard "fly" over each index card. Give a student from each team a flyswatter.

Step 2: When the word on the index card is read aloud, the student with the flyswatter must swat the fly off the card with that word on it, but only if the fly is the same color as their team's color. For example, you could assign orange to Team A, blue to Team B, and so on. Make sure there are equal numbers of flies in each color.

Step 3: To make the game more challenging, use words related to those appearing in the reading. For example, if the passage includes the phrase "swathes of seats stood empty," the teacher could call out the word "audience," and the students would need to justify the connection they made between the word and the passage at the end of the game.

---

136. *Freeze Game*

Type: Warm-up

Materials: Music player, soft music

Step 1: Prepare a passage where few words are repeated. Assign words that are not repeated to students in the class. Instruct the students to freeze when they hear the word they have been given.

Step 2: Play soft music and have the students dance and move around the class. Read the passage. As students hear their words they start to freeze. At the end of the reading of the passage the students still standing have lost the game.

---

137. *Sentence Builder Card Game*

Type: Drilling / Repetition

Materials: Deck of cards

Step 1: Assign parts of speech to each suit. As a guideline, you may decide that:

- Black cards represent verbs, adverbs, and auxiliary verbs.
- Red cards represent nouns, pronouns, articles, and adjectives.

Within that, spades can be verbs and clubs can be adverbs, for example.

Step 2: Deal out 5 cards to each student and have them build sentences using the cards in their hands.

Step 3: They should write a key and place the cards in the correct order to form a grammatically correct sentence. The student who puts together the highest number of correct combinations wins the game.

138. Hot Seat

Type: Drilling / Repetition

Materials: Index cards

Step 1: The student in the hot seat, facing the class, looks at an index card. It will have a main word on it and several related words in smaller fonts below.

Step 2: The student in the hot seat must get the class to guess the main word without using any of the related words.

---

139. Talking Balloons

Type: Repetition / Drilling

Materials: Balloons

Step 1: Write a list of verbs on the board in the infinitive and a simple sentence containing that verb. List all the tenses in English on the board as well.

Step 2: Have students pair up. Each pair should have a balloon to tap between each other and keep aloft. When the student taps the balloon, they repeat the first sentence in the first tense listed. Their partner will tap the balloon back to them and repeat the same sentence in the next tense listed. They will move down the list of tenses with the correct forms of the first verb until they reach the end of the list of tenses.

Step 3: Then, still tapping the balloon between them, they will move on to the next verb on the board.

The trick is not to let the balloon fall but to tap it back and say the next sentence at the same time, correctly and in sequence.

---

140. Dice Games

Type: Repetition / Drilling

Materials: None

Step 1: Write out six grammar structures on the board. Assign each structure to a number from one to six. Throw the die and when it lands on any number have the student repeat the sentence with the grammar structure for that sentence. For example,

1 = "They learned from him."

2 = "Why behave in that way?"

3 = "Before we realized it, the show had ended."

4 = "Opening the gate was the best decision we could have made."

5 = "Besides the discipline, he enjoys the structure."

6 = "For all his faults, he is very generous."

Step 2: When the die lands on 2, for instance, the student must repeat the grammar structure but change one word.

Step 3: Immediately roll the die again and have the student repeat the next sentence, again with only one word changed.

141. *What's This?*

Type: Drilling / Repetition

Materials: Index cards

Step 1: Add new words to the vocabulary using double-sided index cards. For instance, on one side, place a picture of a cloud, and on the reverse side, the word "cumulonimbus". Similarly, on one side, place a picture of a tree, and on the other side, a word like "coniferous" or "deciduous". Keep changing the pictures and the words as spelling and comprehension are mastered.

Step 2: To begin with, introduce the vocabulary by showing students the cards one after the other.

Step 3: Then, hold up the pictures and ask the students to write down the corresponding words. Review by checking the spelling of the words.

Team-based Games

142. *Lost In A Jungle*

Type: Team-based

Materials: None

Step 1: Assign students to groups of no less than three but no more than six. Have a list prepared of 20 small items that people may or may not need if they're lost in the jungle. Write your list on the board.

Step 2: Each group may decide on 5 items on the list which they all agree are essential. This is a good exercise in debate.

Creative students may pick items that seem irrelevant and then convince everyone of its many uses so that everyone understands their logic. Most students have a struggle convincing others and narrowing down only five items.

---

143. *Sketches*

Type: Team-based

Materials: Paper and pencil

Step 1: Pair students. Sketch a scenario: a crime has been committed and the suspect is in the room. Each student must take a turn to choose who they suspect from amongst their classmates.

Step 2: They must then describe the features of the suspect to their partner. The partner, in turn, without knowing who is suspect is, should draw the features being described.

Step 3: When the mugshots are complete, the artist should try to guess who in the room they have just drawn a picture of. Particularly good sketches can be shown to the class for them to guess at.

---

144.   *Mini Plays*

Type: Team-based

Materials: None

Step 1: Choose a piece of dialogue from a play or write your own. It can be something that builds suspense, like the example below:

Mom: "I don't know why you feel you have to do this."

Jody: "I love you mom."

Mom: "Your father will miss you."

Jody: "Won't you?"

Mom: "I've packed some food and other things for you. Be safe, okay?"

Step 2: Pair the students. They may choose their roles and create a play that dramatizes what happens next. Give them five minutes to practice, and then they can present their plays to the class.

---

145. _Movie Review_

MOVIE REVIEW

MOVIE TITLE

MAIN ACTION

Type: Team-based

Materials: None

Step 1: Divide students into groups of no more than four and have them choose a favourite movie, cartoon, or series to review. In their review, they should talk about the central plot, any sub-plots they noticed, and the performances of the actors. They should provide a synopsis and justify their choice of picture.

Step 2: After discussing and editing their review, they can present it to the class in the form of a talk show. The group should play the roles of an actor, director, and critic for the film, who are interviewed as a panel by an anchor.

Step 3: They should also give their final review in for marking and correction by the teacher. The review can include pictures to enhance their presentation.

---

146.   *The Miming Game*

Type: Team-based

Materials: None

Step 1: Pair students and give each pair a set of sentences, each with an underlined word to be mimed. The pairs should compete against each other to identify the most underlined words. For example:

"Who else would already have finished their <u>Christmas</u> shopping?"

Step 2: Have one in the pair mime the word "Christmas" while the other tries to guess it.

---

147.   *General Knowledge*

Type: Team-based

Materials: None

Step 1: Divide a sheet of paper into columns and label each column with a category: NAME, PLACE, COUNTRY, ANIMAL, PLANT, FRUIT/VEGETABLE, and TOTAL.

Step 2: Then, select a category and have each team write down items belonging to that category from A to Z.

Step 3: When the first student in each team completes their list, they should shout "STOP," and everyone should stop writing in that category and move on to the next category.

The student with the most words for the entire game wins, but points should be deducted if students write down the same words.

---

148. *A-Z Race*

Type: Team-based

Materials: None

Step 1: To revise vocabulary, students can be divided into teams. They can, in the style of a relay race, write words starting with A, then B, then C and all the way to Z on the board in a category.

Step 2: The first student can pick the category. If someone given the marker can't think of a word in that category starting with the next letter, they may leave a space but the team with the most correctly spelled words at the end wins.

---

149. *Debate*

Type: Team-based

Materials: None

Step 1: Ask students for their viewpoints on animals in captivity. Assign two teams of three each to debate for and against on a related statement.

Example: ***A lion mauls a tourist.***

Step 2: Get the students to role-play and then debate the following incident:

Two tourists put their heads out of the car in a South African game park to take close-up pictures of a lion hunting. The lion attacked one of them and tried to drag them from the car. The tourist was injured. Visitors are strictly prohibited from putting their heads and hands out of their vehicle windows.

Step 3: Debate: Should the lions be put down? Should game parks house lions in the first place?

---

150. *Flip A Card*

Type: Team-based

Materials: Standard deck of playing cards

Step 1: For each card from ace to king, assign two letters of the alphabet, and write these on the board. For example:

Ace	2	3	4	5	6	7	8	9	10	J	Q	K
A	B	C	D	E	F	G	H	I	J	K	L	M
N	O	P	Q	R	S	T	U	V	W	X	Y	Z

Step 2: Flip seven cards at a time. Each student should write a sentence using only the words beginning with the given letters, in order. Students can read their sentences aloud.

---

151. *The Exclusive*

Type: Team-based

Materials: None

Step 1: Assign students to the roles of editor, photographer, accountant, mother of a victim (also a journalist), and other journalists from other sections of the newspaper.

Scenario: A serious newspaper, trying to employ 50 people, mostly parents, is on the verge of closure. It gets what seems to be a break when it receives a graphic photo of the injured and dead lining the scene of a major accident on a nearby highway. The accident involved a school bus and several cars. The accident happened in heavy fog. The picture is shocking, and the team debate whether to put the picture on the front page.

Step 2: Preparation: Each student can profile their character and their motivations. When the informal debate is over, collect the main arguments raised, and write them down on the board.

Step 3: As a class, discuss the arguments to fully evaluate their logic and validity.

---

152. *Comprehension Test*

Type: Team-based

Materials: Comprehension reading

Step 1: Students are divided into groups and asked to read a passage. They are then asked to generate questions that can be answered by carefully studying the text. Each group should also write down the answers to their questions.

Step 2: The groups then exchange their texts and question sheets with another group, who must answer the questions within a specified time limit.

Points are awarded to groups who answer correctly within the given timeframe.

---

153. *Broken Telephone*

Type: Team-based

Materials: None

Step 1: Divide the class into two and line the students up. Whisper a message in the ear of the student at the end of the line. Whisper the same message to the student at the end of the other line.

Step 2: Have each student whisper the message they receive into the ear of the person next to them until the last player gets the message.

Step 3: The last player should present the message loudly for the entire class to hear.

The first team to correctly repeat the message out loud at the end wins.

---

154. *Naughts & Crosses*

Type: Team-based

Materials: None

Step 1: Put a naughts-and-crosses grid on the board. Number the blocks from one to nine. Have nine revision questions prepared.

Step 2: Divide the class into two teams. One team is X and the other O. Each team will take a turn to call out a number and then they will be asked the corresponding question.

If the question is correctly answered, then either a naught or a cross will go down in that block for that team. The first team to complete three in a row, horizontally, diagonally, or vertically, wins.

---

155. *Triple Pelmanisms*

Type: Team-based

Materials: Index cards

Step 1: Give each student a set of 36 cards to place upside down in a 6x6 grid or scatter them randomly across the floor.

Step 2: Each player takes turns to uncover three cards at a time, and all players should be able to see the cards. If all three cards match, the set may be kept. If they do not match, they should be returned to the grid.

The cards can contain words or pictures, such as "bathroom," "toilet," and "shower," which would constitute one set. Alternatively, the cards could have verbs in different tenses, such as 'to sink,' 'sank,' and 'would have sunk.' Make sure that the words cannot be read when the cards are upside down. Once all the cards have been claimed, the team with the most sets wins.

---

156. *Round Table*

Type: Team-based

Materials: Index cards, die

Step 1: Place students in circles of no more than six. Deal out a pack of index cards to them. The student who rolls the highest on a die starts.

Step 2: Then then take a card and describe the word on it without saying it. Any of the other students can guess what the word is.

If two students guess simultaneously, they must flip a coin or roll a die to decide who wins the card. At the end of the game, the one with the most wins.

Spelling and Grammar

157. *Hear And Jump*

Type: Spelling

Materials: None

Step 1: Find a story in which the same words appear frequently. Read the first two or three sentences of the passage and assign the words in there to students.

Step 2: Every time their word is read the student must jump up and quickly sit down again.

Adults may prefer just marking a piece of paper. For more advanced students, you may be able to give them letters to listen for, which tests spelling. It also works well to get advanced students to listen for the frequency of certain consonant or vowel sounds.

---

158. *Preposition Practice*

Type: Spelling/ Grammar

Materials: None

Step 1: Prepare a text that contains prepositions and remove all the prepositions. Print those on a separate piece of paper and cut them out into flash cards. Put the flashcards in an envelope. Prepare one envelope per group.

Step 2: Assign students to different groups and give each group one envelope. Read the text you have prepared and tell the students that whenever you raise your hand one person from their team must put the right preposition on the front desk.

The fastest team to get the correct answer gets the point. The same game could be played with adjectives, articles, and pronouns. This game can be adapted for any level.

Speaking and Pronunciation

159. *Just A Minute*

Type: Turn-based

Materials: None

This game was a wonderfully popular show on BBC radio. It ran for decades. It really tests fluency and quick thinking.

Step 1: Write topics on strips of paper. Good topics may include:

- My greatest pleasure

- Why I am so educated

- The Theory of Everything

- Home renovation

- Natural disasters

- Afternoons spent with relatives

Any topics appropriate for the age and level of the class will do.

Step 2: Have a volunteer come up and remind everyone of the rules of the game. These are, speak for just a minute without repetition, hesitation, or deviation on the topic you pick at random.

Step 3: At this point, allow the volunteer to draw a topic. Start the timer. Let him speak. If another student catches him hesitating, repeating himself or deviating from the topic he can be called out for that.

Step 4: As soon as the speaker is interrupted start the time. Judge whether the interruption was fair. If it was let the person who interrupted continue speaking on the topic in the time remaining. If it was not a fair interruption, ask the original speaker to continue.

The person speaking when the final whistle blows gets one point, and the person who presents the best arguments for each topic gets 2 points.

Memory and Concentration

160.   Grandfathers Will

Type: Concentration/ Memory

Materials: None

Step 1: Students are seated in a circle and each assigned a number, from 1 to 20. Each student must remember his number and ask a question on it. The game might go like this:

No. 1: "When grandfather died, he left us twenty fields of wheat."

No. 20: (This is the only person allowed to answer.) "Why 20? I counted only 14."

No. 14: "I doubt that. Was it not 17?"

No. 17: "No, I remember it was 8."

Step 2: Any student who hesitates when his number is called or makes a mistake must quit the round. This game demands concentration. The last one remaining wins.

---

161. *LipSync Battle*

Type: Concentration/ Memory

Materials: Music player

Step 1: Find songs that are relatively catchy. Assign students to groups of no more than 5. Each group should be given a different song, and all the students should work together to understand the words and meaning of the song.

Step 2: Let the students put on a lip-sync battle, group against group, where they tell a story that expresses the soul of the song.

Turn-based Games

162. Conversation Must Be Kept

Type: Turn-based

Materials: None

Step 1: Start a conversation with a sentence where the first word starts with the first letter of the alphabet.

Step 2: The next person in turn should respond in a meaningful way to your statement or question in one sentence. Their sentence should start with the next letter of the alphabet. The exchange could look like this:

A: "Andy has been ill through most of the summer."

B: "But, I'm sure he is feeling stronger now."

A: "Could that be because of the medication from Doctor…?"

B: "Doctor Nicholson? "

A: "Exactly."

B: "For as long as I've known him, he has been a strange man but an excellent doctor."

And so on…

163. The Art Of Lying

Type: Turn-based

Materials: Whiteboard/ paper

Step 1: Ask students to write three statements about themselves on a piece of paper. Two should be true and the other one false.

Step 2: Pair them. One partner should ask the other questions about each statement and then guess which one is true. Students should switch partners and keep playing. For example:

- "I am allergic to shellfish."

- "I've had cosmetic surgery."

- "My middle name is Hubert."

Step 3: When the game is over let the students take turns to announce one thing they learned about a classmate in the game.

---

164. *What's The Trouble?*

Type: Turn-based

Materials: Post-it notes

Step 1: Write down an illness or a problem from a recent class on a post-it note. Stick post-it notes on the back of each student.

Step 2: Allow them to walk around the class asking for advice from one another to solve their problem. They should find enough advice to guess what their problem might be, based on what they are told.

Use more obscure or complex problems for more advanced students. For lower levels, let them know the types of problems to expect in advance.

---

165. *Peace And Order*

Type: Turn-based

Materials: None

If a class is really getting much too boisterous and out of hand this game may help to restore order.

Step 1: Each student should write down at least three things they would like to see changed in the classroom and write an essay on how these changes would benefit the class.

Step 2: Ask students to write down the pros and cons of dispensing with rules completely and to present their perspectives.

---

166.   *Stories From The Wild*

Type: Turn-based

Materials: None

Step 1: Let a student start to tell a story of themselves as an animal. The next student can expand on the story adding details about the setting. The following student can describe some action that occurred. The next in line can describe a turning point for the main animal character.

Step 2: The game can also function as a dialogue between animals, with each student taking on the role of the animal they chose.

---

167.   *Saved By The Bell*

Type: Turn-based

Materials: Bell, waste basket, ball

Step 1: Put the bell or buzzer inside the wastebasket and get a student to toss the ball into the basket.

Step 2: If he gets it right and the ball hits the buzzer and it rings, he is "saved by the bell". If he doesn't hear the bell, he must answer an awkward question.

Prepare cards beforehand with as many awkward questions as possible. Some examples of awkward questions may be:

• When did you last lie to your mother?

- What was the last item you stole?

- What is your nickname? and so on.

---

168. *Bragging Game*

Type: Turn-based

Materials: None

Step 1: Write out between twenty and thirty sentences in the present perfect tense that describes an activity that grants bragging rights. For example: "I've traveled to over 30 countries." "I've climbed Mount Everest."

Step 2: Students will each select a slip of paper with an outrageous brag. They will read it aloud, and their teammates will attempt to outdo them with a more impressive and outrageous statement than the last. For example:

A: "I've flown in a private jet."

B: "I've flown in a private jet owned by a celebrity."

C: "I've flown a private jet owned by a celebrity."

D: "I own a private jet that a celebrity borrows from me."

E: "Do you know who I am? I'm the person who sold that celebrity their private jet."

Step 3: When they cannot come up with anything better, they can say "Wow, good for you" and proceed to the next brag. Remember to spell-check for any errors.

---

169. Time Indicators

Type: Turn-based

Materials: None

Step 1: Write each tense on the board.

Step 2: Have each student take a turn to start a sentence in that tense and have another finish it. It is useful to keep track of the verbs used. Verbs may only be used once. The game may go like this:

A: "At this moment in time, . . ."

B: ". . . I am sitting in a classroom."

B: "Last year at this time I would have . . ."

C: ". . . been in Europe."

C: "Every day for the past month. . ."

D: ". . . she has taken a taxi to work."

---

170. Mallet

Type: Turn-based

Materials: Soft toy mallet

Step 1: Put two chairs back-to-back at the front of the class. Have two students volunteer to sit on them. The first student must say a word and the other must say a related word.

Step 2: They should keep taking turns to say related words to the first word spoken but once a word has been used, it cannot be reused. No two words can be said simultaneously.

For any violation of these rules, the mallet will touch a student on the head.

---

171.   *English Jeopardy*

Type: Turn-based

Materials: None

Step 1: Select four or five categories from the textbook and draw a scorecard like the one below.

Step 2: Divide the class into teams or let them work individually. Each in turn may select a category of question and a score to play for.

Multiple Choice | Sentence Builder | True/False | Missing Word

---

100

_____

200

_____

300

_____

172. _Adverbial Charades_

Type: Turn-based

Materials: None

Step 1: Give students adverb flashcards and ask them to mime an action so that the class can guess the adverb on their card.

173. _Demonstration_

Type: Turn-based

Materials: None

Step 1: Prepare slips of paper with instructions like these:

- You're driving home in anger after you receive some bad news. A person runs into the road in front of you…

- The ring with which you will propose to your partner has slipped down the sewer.

- Your new boss is the someone you used to bully at school, etc.

Step 2: Give each student a slip of paper and have them act out the action silently for the entire class to guess. The first to correctly guess in English wins the round.

---

174. *Minute Man*

Type: Turn-based

Materials: 30 seconds cards

Step 1: Team students up and hand them a stack of cards. Flip a coin to decide which side of the card to use.

Step 2: Pick a player in the team and ask them not to describe but to impersonate each of the famous people/places on the card. When the rest of the team guesses they may move on.

Allow each player a turn of 60 seconds. They earn one point for every correctly guessed character.

---

175. *Billionaire*

Type: Turn-based

Materials: Monopoly money may be useful

Step 1: Assign "prize-money" to the digits 0-9.

Step 2: Have students answer questions and review the answers. If the students answer a question correctly and the amount assigned to the corresponding digit is $1,000, the student wins $1,000. However, if the students answer a question incorrectly and the amount assigned to the corresponding digit is $200,000, the student will lose $200,000.

---

176. *Show Down*

Type: Turn-based

Materials: Index cards

Step 1: Divide the class into teams. Ask a question to one team. Reveal the answer after the team has responded.

Step 2: If the question is correctly answered the team wins a point. If not, the other team may attempt the question to win the point.

---

177.   *Performance Fit*

Type: Turn-based

Materials: None

Step 1: Write a list of popular songs on the board. Have students pick a song they know particularly well and practice it.

Step 2: In turns they can come to the front and silently perform the song, as though they were doing a lip-sync.

The student will be silent throughout their performance. Their knowledge of the words and interpretation of the song will score them points.

---

178.   *Steal, Swap, Bust, And Number*

Type: Turn-based

Materials: None

Step 1: Make a copy of the grid below and cut it into cards. Put the cards in a hat and shuffle them. Divide the class into two teams. Flip a coin to decide who starts.

Step 2: The first team is asked a question. It should be a review question or question from a 'Word Up' question sheet. If the student who started cannot answer, a teammate can help. When the question is answered, the team draws a card. The cards work as follows:

Numbers: If the card has a number, that number is added to the team's score.

Steal: If the card says "Steal," the team who drew the card adds all the opposition's points to their score and leaves the opposition on zero.

Bust: If the card "Bust" is drawn, the team's score reverts to zero.

Swap: The teams' scores must swap. If Team A has 200 points and Team B only 100, then the scores will invert. Team A will be left with 100, and Team B will have 200.

Steal, Swap, Bust and Number

Steal	Bust	Swap
Steal	Bust	Swap
Steal	Bust	Swap
Steal	Bust	Swap
100	0	50
80	70	40
10	5	20
1	60	90
95	0	55

One-one-One Games

179. *Animals For A Day*

Type: One-on-one

Materials: A list of different animals

Step 1: Ask students to choose an animal from the list silently.

Step 2: Have them write a journal describing their day as that animal.

The students who write the most imaginative stories win.

---

180. *Career Letters*

Type: One-on-one (Or as a class)

Materials: None

Step 1: Ask students to choose a career they are interested in pursuing and write to a school about it. Their letter should request information about how they can pursue their chosen field.

Step 2: When their letters are complete, help them to perfect it and post them.

Share the replies from the various schools with the class.

---

181.   *Who Am I?*

Type: One-on-one (Or as a class)

Materials: None

Step 1: Write the names of famous people (current or historical) on cards and tape them to the foreheads of each student. No one should see the name taped to their foreheads.

Step 2: They can walk around the class and have others show only by subtle, nuanced remarks what their impression of the personality is. Students may ask questions about the person on their forehead, but other students may only respond with subtle clues and hints. No explanations or direct answers should be given.

This activity can be a fun and interactive way for students to learn about historical or current figures while practicing their communication and critical thinking skills.

---

182.   *Guess The Picture*

Type: One-on-one (Or as a class)

Materials: Index cards with pictures of famous photos or artworks

Step 1: Prepare cards with pictures on them of famous photos or artworks.

Step 2: One student can select a card and describe features of the picture without giving any indication of how they are composed.

Step 3: The other students have the challenge to guess which picture is being described.

---

183. *The Opening Sequence*

Type: One-on-one (Or as a class)

Materials: Video player, advertisement, or photo montage

Step 1: Show a fast-moving montage that includes many people, objects, and actions. A cable television advertisement would work well for this activity.

Step 2: Ask the students to list as many things as they can in a particular category shown in the frames. Play the sequence at normal speed and do not allow them to take notes.

Step 3: Afterwards, allow them to re-watch the sequence slowly frame by frame and tick off the items they see on the list.

Points are deducted for items they wrote that are not in the frames. The categories can be "items starting with M", "environments", "equipment", "actions", "people", or any other category that you choose.

---

184. *Fishing For English*

Type: One-on-one (Or as a class)

Materials: None

Step 1: As a weekend homework assignment, ask students to look for words from magazine advertisements in their own language that are derived from English.

Step 2: A montage of these words can then be created and placed on the classroom wall as a visual display.

---

185. *Kim's Game*

Type: One-on-one (Or as a class)

Materials: Miscellaneous jumble

Step 1: Place various items on a desk and cover them with a cloth. Ask students to observe and remember the objects on the desk. After 3 minutes, remove the cloths and allow the students to see the objects again.

Step 2: Have students write down all the objects they saw.

Step 3: Check the objects ticked off the lists, and deduct points for any items written down that were not on the desk.

The winner is the student who correctly remembers and identifies the English names for the most items.

---

186. *Making Headlines*

Type: One-on-one (Or as a class)

Materials: 40-word cut-outs

Step 1: Cut out 40 words from an English newspaper or magazine, ensuring a fair and balanced sample of different parts of speech.

Step 2: Hand out a few copies of the words out to the class, and have the students work in teams or individually have the students make grammatically correct sentences using the words.

Step 3: Time the activity and ask students to create 5 sentences with 5 words each, or 3 sentences with 3, 5, and 7 words respectively. Examples of sentences include:

"Radio is happy" (3 words)

"All MPs are cows" (4 words)

"Scientists enjoy lunch in summer" (5 words)

Step 4: After creating sentences, encourage students to use them to write a story or news article, as if they were headlines.

---

187. Spin

Type: One-on-one (Or as a class)

Materials: None

Step 1: Spin a wheel marked with numbers. When the marker stops on a segment, ask a question from the textbook or a 'Word Up' question sheet and award points.

This game can be played with teams, a whole class, or in one-on-one instruction.

---

188. Snakes & Ladders - Adverbs

Type: One-on-one (Or as a class)

Materials: Snakes & Ladders board game, die, chips

Step 1: The player who rolls the highest number on the die starts. They should roll again to move forward.

Step 2: Each block should be pre-populated with flashcards of adverbs.

Step 3: When a student lands on an adverb block, they should write down as many appropriate verbs as they can to go with that adverb.

As a variation, the student must make sentences with the adverb of the same number as the die they rolled. For example, if the student rolled a 5 and lands on "merrily", they must make 5 sentences with the word "merrily".

---

189.   _Snakes & Ladders - Future Tense_

Type: One-on-one (Or as a class)

Materials: Snakes & Ladders board game, die, chips

Step 1: Pre-populate each block with flashcards of verbs. The student who rolls the highest starts. Roll again to move forward.

Step 2: When a student lands on a verb they must make a sentence of that verb in the future tense.

---

190.   _Snakes & Ladders - Non Stop Questions_

Type: One-on-one (Or as a class)

Materials: Snakes & Ladders board game, die, chips

Step 1: The student who rolls the highest on the die starts. Roll again to move forward.

Step 2: If the student lands on 4, they must answer question 4 in a textbook review. If they land on 32, they must answer question 32 and so forth.

---

191. *Riddle, Riddle*

THE BIG BOOK OF

FUN RIDDLES & JOKES

DAVID CHASE

Type: One-on-one (Or as a class)

Materials: *The Big Book of Fun Riddles & Jokes*

Step 1: Download a free copy of "*The Big Book of Fun Riddles & Jokes*".

Step 2: Create a game using the riddles by asking a riddle from the book and awarding points in a quiz-like format.

This game can be played with teams, the whole class, or in one-on-one instruction.

Step 3: To make the game more engaging, you can also add a time limit for answering each riddle or include some physical challenges for the teams to complete as they answer the riddles. You can also encourage students to come up with their own riddles and add them to the game.

Please Don't Forget...

Thank you for choosing one of our books! We know you have lots of wonderful options out there, and your patronage means the world to our small publishing company.

Please share your experience on Amazon

We hope you have a memorable journey with this book. We would be happy to receive your feedback which helps us improve and bring more educational books to our audiences, and helps future buyers to make confident decisions.

To leave an Amazon review please visit https://www.amazon.com/ryp or scan the QR code below...

DON'T FORGET YOUR BONUS BOOK!

We are delighted to offer you a complimentary and exclusive copy of "*The Big Book of Fun Riddles & Jokes*." This resource is specifically designed to help English teachers make the most of their class time by engaging students in thought-provoking, interactive activities.

We understand that every moment of class time is precious, and that's why we've curated a collection of quick-fire riddles and brain teasers that will encourage your students to learn English while having fun. By incorporating these activities into your lessons, you can create a dynamic and stimulating learning environment that will keep your students focused and motivated.

To access your free copy of "*The Big Book of Fun Riddles & Jokes*," simply click on the following link:
https://www.subscribepage.com/davidchase. We highly recommend that you take advantage of this opportunity to enhance your teaching skills and inspire your students to achieve their full potential.

Printed in Great Britain
by Amazon

37357749R00096